TOO MANY PEOPLE

The Case for Reversing Growth

LINDSEY GRANT

SEVEN LOCKS PRESS

Santa Ana, California
Minneapolis, Minnesota
Washington, D.C.

Seven Locks Press
P.O. Box 25689
Santa Ana, CA 92799
(800) 354-5348

Individual Sales. This book is available through most bookstores or can be ordered directly from Seven Locks Press at the address above.

Quantity Sales. Special discounts are available on quantity purchases by corporations, associations, and others. For details, contact the "Special Sales Department" at the publisher's address above.

Printed in the United States of America

Library of Congress Cataloging-in-Publication Data
is available from the publisher
ISBN 0-929765-93-1 (cloth)
ISBN 0-929765-91-5 (paper)

Cover and interior design and production by Sparrow Advertising & Design

This book is dedicated to the two-child family.

About the Author

LINDSEY GRANT writes on population and public policy. A retired Foreign Service Officer, he was a China specialist and served as Director of the Office of Asian Communist Affairs, National Security Council staff member, and Department of State Policy Planning Staff member.

As Deputy Assistant Secretary of State for Environment and Population Affairs, he was Department of State coordinator for the *Global 2000 Report to the President*, Chairman of the interagency committee on International Environmental Affairs, United States delegate to (and Vice Chairman of) the OECD Environment Committee and United States member of the UN ECE Committee of Experts on the Environment.

His books includes *Juggernaut: Growth on a Finite Planet, Foresight and National Decisions: The Horseman and the Bureaucrat, Elephants in the Volkswagen* (a study of optimum United States population) and *How Many Americans?*

CONTENTS

FIGURES

ACKNOWLEDGEMENTS

This book was originally written as a handbook for Negative Population Growth, Inc., to make the case as to why a population turnaround is very badly needed, in the United States and most of the rest of the world. I am appreciative that James Riordan and Seven Locks Press have undertaken to offer it to a broader audience.

I wish to thank Donald Mann of Negative Population Growth for his enthusiastic support of the project, and David Simcox, Bud Sperry, and Richard Maxwell for their helpful advice and editing as the text progressed.

Lindsey Grant
Santa Fe, New Mexico
September 2000

I. THE ISSUE AT HAND

They say the Demilitarized Zone in Korea, which had long been a barren region, has reverted to a lovely young hardwood forest since it was freed from the human footprint by the 1953 armistice agreement. It is an unexpected and accidental commentary on the role of man in nature. In this age of human dominance, we inadvertently destroy the natural systems that support us, and it is only by chance that we are suddenly aware of what we have done.

Our future depends on learning to come into better balance with the rest of nature and to find a sustainable relationship we have yet to achieve. To pose the issue as a more somber question: is the present course of human activities consistent with the preservation of the Earth's existing life support systems? In this essay, I will survey the current evidence and make the case that we can turn the present deteriorating system around only by ending the worldwide infatuation with growth and embracing the idea of a return to a smaller population.

Just as perpetual growth in a finite space is a mathematical absurdity, its reversal becomes equally absurd if carried too far, except for those who would applaud the disappearance of the human race. The reversal of growth (negative population growth or NPG) to my mind is the ideal of a turnaround in world and United States population until we approach a less destructive and more tolerable level, perhaps at numbers the United States and the world passed two or more generations ago.

Europe's population growth is on the verge of turning around, and the almost universal reaction has been panic at the prospect—as if the population it so recently attained is essential to its survival. The reaction illuminates the general infatuation with growth. Few questions were raised as population grew, but the end of growth is seen as a disaster. I will argue later that a smaller European population would be good for Europe and the world.

Humans since the Neolithic age have been proficient at disturbing and displacing natural systems, notably through forest destruction, land erosion and species extinction. With the advent of the industrial revolution, we have multiplied our disturbance as we extract minerals from the air and the Earth's crust, invent new chemicals and dump them all heedlessly into the biosphere. Now we are on the threshold of adding genetic manipulation—deliberately redesigning animals and plants—that may be as destabilizing as the earlier two revolutions. We are changing the Earth without having demonstrated that we know how to manage it.

There is something new on Earth: human systems have grown to the point at which the damage we do has become intolerable, not only to other species, but to our own future. As our problems have been caused or compounded by the growth of populations and economic activity, their solution requires that we turn growth around.

This book will explore several sectors where human activity is pressing hard against the environment. I will attempt to sort out how much the impacts can be mitigated by technology or changing behavior and to what degree a population decline or stabilization is essential to success. I will focus on present trends in world population, economic activity, food, water, energy and climate, chemicals and pollution, and loss of biodiversity. In some of these areas, one can roughly quantify population levels that would make a solution possible. They come out in the one to three billion range. In others, such as climate and energy, so much depends on mankind's ability and willingness to embrace technical solutions that a desirable population number cannot be offered—it is a two-part calculation that involves balancing numbers and behavior. In none of the areas, be it noted, can it reasonably be argued that a larger population helps in finding solutions.

If I seem to belabor the population connection, bear with me. All these issues have a self-evident connection to population growth. I find it astonishing that the technical literature seldom touches upon that connection and never—almost literally never—mentions population policy as part of the solution. (I did a search of the literature for the 1997 United Nations (UN) General Assembly session on sustainability, and it was a disheartening proof of that point.[1]

II. POPULATION AND MIGRATION

Very briefly, let me describe where population growth stands now and underline its connection with this Age of Migrations.

Population. The United States' population was 75 million in 1900. It is now about 275 million. It may well grow to 404 million by 2050 and 571 million in 2100. (Census 1999 middle projection). Post-2000 immigrants and their descendants will contribute two-thirds of that growth.

For the world, the UN estimates are 1.6 billion in 1900, 6 billion now, with 8.9 billion projected for 2050 and about 10 billion in 2100 (medium projections, 1998). Like most estimates and projections, they embody many assumptions and sheer guesses and should be read as general trend indicators rather than fixed truths.

This remarkable worldwide growth masks two totally different trends in the "developed" and "less developed" countries. The industrial ("developed") countries other than the United States presently have less than 10 percent of world population, and this percentage is dropping fast because their fertility has declined dramatically. Their populations either are already declining or will begin to decline in the next few decades. Some "newly industrializing countries" are coming to resemble those old industrial countries: low fertility, declining population growth, aging populations, high living standards and the attendant pollution. They are a growing and ill-defined group, which includes Korea, Taiwan, Malaysia, and Singapore.

Similar changes are happening in the urban sector of countries such as China, India, and Brazil, but not enough to transform those countries. They still share the curses of the less developed countries (LDCs): forest destruction and land degradation, competition for water, high levels of disease, low productivity, low wages, and high unemployment.

Overall, LDC population is rising by 75 million people a year. It is expected to rise some 73 percent in the next half-century and comprise 87 percent of world population by 2050, despite the fertility declines in the transitional countries. The poorest of those less developed countries are still the fastest growing despite the inroads of AIDS, and the most desperate.

Although the old definitions of who is "developed" are blurring, this thumbnail sketch suggests that there will be profound implications for migration and for the developed world.

Migration. We are in an Age of Migrations and will be for at least two generations to come. The world is divided by the wage gap. In Mexico, the average hourly wage in manufacturing is (by inflated official estimates) just 10 percent of that in the United States. Elsewhere, gaps are even wider. It is an invitation to migrate. Migrants are helped by employers in the developed countries who are seeking cheap labor to meet the competition of the low-wage countries and of each other. Those employers in turn are in conflict with common folk who see their wages threatened by the import of cheap goods and the export of jobs. The rising anti-immigrant mood in Europe, the riots against the World Trade Organization in Seattle, are only the beginning of this conflict. The tensions are social as well as economic, and they will almost certainly continue to mount. The UN projections treat international migration as a minor and diminishing phenomenon. That is an optimistic appraisal.

> *The migration pressure is a product of overcrowding on the land, of unemployment and wage differentials, all of which are driven by population growth. Those driving forces would subside if somehow the growth should stop or turn around.*

Naturally, poor countries would like to be richer, and some of them are on their way. Mathematically, world gross national product (GNP) would have to rise nearly tenfold in the next century for the projected third world population to reach the affluence of a mid-level industrial nation, which is an explicit target of countries like China and India. The tenfold figure assumes that the existing industrial economies will stop growing, which none of them plan to do.

Indeed, real gross domestic product (GDP) in the United States has been growing in recent years at 3.2 percent per year. That is a doubling every 22 years—sixteen fold growth in 88 years, if such a torrid pace could be maintained. The European Union's economy has been growing at 2.4 percent annually. And yet political leaders in both places, when faced with an economic problem, call for more growth.

> *The whole world is engaged in a pell-mell race to grow faster—driving toward an impossible objective. It is a daunting prospect: the idea of a race to increase economic activity in a world already under stress.*

Take note, however, of one ray of hope. Europe has a lower gross growth rate than the United States but a higher per capita growth, because its population is not growing. Europe may not need such growth, but it is a lesson for poor nations trying to escape poverty.

The GNP Hang-up. The pursuit of GNP growth is a curiously misdirected focus. The economic benefits (such as they are) result from rising per capita income, not the GNP. But the pursuit of higher per capita income is limited in turn by a mighty reality that economists usually ignore: the economy operates only within the environment, even as it transforms the environment. The entire economic enterprise, if it is to survive, must operate within the constraints of environmental sustainability.

> *The only way to reconcile the economic objective with the environmental constraint is to keep total economic activity within tolerable environmental limits. That is, decide first how large a pie the environment can tolerate. Then decide how big the individual slices (the standard of living) should be. Then divide the pie by the size of each slice. The result is the number of slices (the population) the system can support.*

Growth thus defined is a tolerable objective—but it is not overall growth. And it requires a population policy, which means a consensus as to how many people can live comfortably within the environment and a plan for persuading people to stay within that constraint.

Inverting Growth. Now, let us turn the calculation around. Ask not how much economic growth will be needed to support a growing population in dignity; ask instead how many people could live at a decent level at the present rates of economic activity. Hold your hat. If we take the average per capita GNP of the World Bank's forty-four "high income" countries as a crude surrogate for a good standard of living, and if we assume for the moment that the current world GNP is environmentally sustainable, then a total world population of just 1.06 billion—one-sixth the present world population—could enjoy the generally comfortable standard of living we associate with the industrial countries.[2]

My environmental assumption is generous. In fact, the current level of world GNP, the way we produce it, is not sustainable, judging by the damage we are doing. However, I will assume that at that level of prosperity we can afford to exchange our more damaging activity for more benign practices that would stop the environmental damage, while still maintaining the quality of life. This does not mean giving up modern conveniences, but the hypothetical one billion people would be practicing more efficient ways of providing their light, heat and cooling, and of moving themselves and their goods.

> *The above calculation is one way of approximating a figure for a desirable future population: one billion. Deduct 50 percent for contingencies, if you wish, or add a billion or so on the grounds that benign new technologies will support more people without harming the environment, or that happiness isn't measured completely by GNP.*

I cannot pretend to much precision in this sort of thing, but one thing is clear: the number is much smaller than present world population, and farther yet from the direction we are heading. The calculation is rough for several reasons. Most obviously: GNP growth tends to measure things we did not have to pay for before the growth (like clean air or space to park your car); so a smaller population would not need so much GNP per capita, and it could avoid the environmental costs inherent in high levels of economic activity.

That population figure of one billion is hardly achievable within less than a couple of centuries, barring a natural catastrophe driven perhaps by our own activity. And desirable may not yet be practicable, but certainly a worldwide vote would show that an overwhelming majority of people would like to live that way.

GNP is not the real issue, however; it is simply shorthand for the real question: what is happening to the scale and character of economic activity? What is that doing to our support base and our own future? Moving away from GNP with all its deficiencies as a measure of well being, let us look at the real issues, the implied resource consumption rates and the pollution dangers.

Grains are the backbone of the human diet, whether we eat them directly or feed them to livestock. Grain production is beginning to lose the race with population. Figure 1 tells the story. It is too early to say with confidence whether total production has peaked, but production per capita peaked in the mid-1980s. Before then, the trend permitted some overall improvement in diet by feeding more grain to livestock. The 400 kg figure boxed in the graph is about the level needed to support a decent diet, such as in Italy or Taiwan. People in the poorest countries average about half that consumption level, and they are the ones who are actually losing ground. In Africa, grain production per capita has fluctuated, but in 1997–99 it was less than 90 percent of 1969–71.[3]

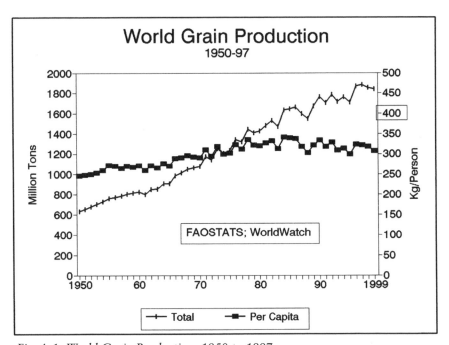

Fig. 4–1. World Grain Production, 1950 to 1997

In the industrial countries, we hardly notice the trend. Europeans and Japanese have long been used to inflated food prices, supported by government policy. World grain prices rose sharply in 1995 because of a bad year in major producing areas and low stockpiles, but the cost of the basic grain is only a tiny share of the price of the food we buy. Corn flakes are a remarkable example. For brand name corn flakes in the United States, about 2 percent goes to the farmer for the corn. The rest of the money goes toward processing, packaging, shipping, merchandising, profits and, above all, advertising.

Need and the ability to buy have become disconnected. Pre-World War II Egypt, when its population was one-third what it is now, was a net exporter of grain. Today, despite awesome gains in yields, it depends on imports for nearly half of its consumption and is hard pressed for the foreign exchange to buy it. And Egypt's population is still rising 1.9 percent per year. United States aid has helped Egypt pay for imported grain, but the rich cannot solve the food problem of the poor nations. If Americans ate less meat and thereby cut United States per capita grain consumption in half (down to the 400 kg level described above), that would free about 5 percent of world production for others to consume— if they could afford to buy it.

Fertilizer. Even more important than the race itself is the way it is run. The world is caught in a trap. It produces more and more commercial fertilizer to grow more food for more people. Worldwide fertilizer use rose six times from 25 million nutrient tons in 1960 to 150 million tons in 1990 and it may rise to 225 million tons by 2020.

Farmers face a diminishing response curve. They get less and less output per pound of fertilizer as they use more of it, so fertilizer use increases faster than food output until it doesn't produce enough food to pay for itself. That saturation point has been reached with major crops in the industrial world; grain yields and fertilizer use are static. To cite two important examples: corn yields in the United States have fluctuated between 6.3 and 8.7 tons per hectare for a decade; rice yields in Japan have hovered around 4.5 tons since 1984, despite an artificial price five times higher than the world level. The predicted increase in fertilizer use by 2020 will be almost entirely in the less developed countries, and it will go on after 2020, because they are still far from being saturated. They may, however, not be able to afford so much fertilizer if energy prices rise, because fertilizer is highly energy-intensive.

Commercial nitrate fertilizer is made by extracting nitrogen from the air, where it is in an inert molecular state, and converting it into soluble and chemically highly active forms. Phosphates, sulfates, and potash are also mined and put into the biosphere. Fertilizers pose a fundamental dilemma. They provide nutrients necessary to life and are therefore good, but in other forms, they can be deadly. Phosphates are used in manufacturing animal poison and nerve gas, and lead sulfates are highly toxic. As they move through the environment, those chemicals can have highly ambivalent personalities. But they are being introduced into a world that was in balance, and too much of even a good thing can be deadly. We find that the environment cannot handle all that fertilizer, but we cannot stop.

We know some of the immediate effects: health problems from nitrates in drinking water: leaching of nutrients from forest soils, acidification of lakes, eutrophication of lakes and bays, leading to oxygen starvation and catastrophic declines in fishery, to "brown slime" in the Adriatic, the "dead zone" in the Gulf of Mexico off New Orleans, and deadly "mahogany tides" in the Chesapeake, all the result of fertilizer runoff.

What we don't know is the cumulative effect of our activity, or the secondary and tertiary effects. Every year, humans put nearly twice as much nitrogen into the biosphere as is created by natural processes, and most of it comes from agriculture. With more to come—every year.

The only reason that nitrogen has not swamped the ecosystem is that certain earth microbes reconvert it into its inert molecular form and send it back into the atmosphere. Like the fertilizers, those microbes are helpful but dangerous. If they succeed too well, they will denitrify the biosphere and starve the world of an input necessary to life. If they fail entirely, the world will be overwhelmed with nitrogen.

All life depends on those microbes, including ours, but we do not really know what keeps their contribution in balance. Can they keep up the good work as the load gets heavier? We don't know much about them or what conditions they need to prosper. A Presidential panel in 1983 raised the possibility that a more acidic environment—the result of energy production from fossil fuels—might kill them (p. 63). We have yet to disprove the panel's warning, yet we keep using more fossil fuel and more fertilizer.

We will continue to unload fertilizers into the environment for the indefinite future. If we stopped, literally billions of people would starve, because nearly half the nitrogen needed to grow crops comes from commercial fertilizer. (Much of the rest is from the cultivation of legumes to fix nitrogen in the soil.) This is not a future problem; we are deep into the trap.

> *We live in an exquisitely balanced ecosystem. We are tampering with that balance in the pursuit of more food production, and we do not know what we are doing.*

There is no way of making the impact of fertilizer more benign other than using it more efficiently—which is already being done in the industrial countries. But if we could tolerate lower yields, we would be out of this squirrel cage. United States corn yields a century ago were a little less than 40 percent of present yields, without commercial fertilizer. Farmers used animal and green manure, mulch and crop rotation, which had the collateral benefit of helping to control pests and weeds. This is a cycling process; it doesn't systematically inject more chemicals into the biosphere.

> *Question: isn't the solution on the demand side? Lower the demand and we need much less fertilizer and thereby escape the trap.*

Much hope and money are invested right now in genetic modification (GM). The ultimate dream is that all major crops (and not just legumes) can be modified to produce their own nitrogen from symbiotic microbes. Beware! If we succeed, it will reduce the transaction costs and incidental pollution of producing nitrogen—we won't need the factories—but it will become easier to load more nitrogen into the biosphere. That dream could become a nightmare as nitrogen in the biosphere multiplies. Moreover, the ability to manufacture nitrogen might escape from crops into related weeds. Such super-weeds might multiply and lead to more nitrogen releases. This is not just a horror story; it is a real possibility. We are learning from AIDS and other medical research that genes can jump from one species to another.

> *Why do we even contemplate taking such a risk with genetic modification? Because our scientists must find ways to provide more food for an expanding world population.*

Pesticides. To maximize yields, we use pesticides and herbicides to eliminate the competition. Then we find that the weeds and pests fight back; they develop resistance to the chemicals. We are not winning. By one estimate, about 50 percent of world crops are still lost to pests and weeds. And the Green Revolution crop varieties tend to be more susceptible than the varieties they replaced.[4] Meanwhile, those poisons poison their users. They have been associated with neurological deterioration, skin problems, reproductive disorders, and cancer. One study in Ecuador found 60 percent of the farm workers showing symptoms of pesticide poisoning, but the national or worldwide impacts cannot be quantified simply for lack of data.[5]

Since the DDT fiasco, science has come up with pesticides and herbicides that are more selective and less long lasting. However, nobody seems to have investigated what the chemicals are transformed into when they degrade, and what the potential consequences are. And nobody is saying, as they did in the 1960s, that we have won our war with the bugs and weeds. Genetic modification will add another weapon to our arsenal, but again bugs and weeds are fighting back, and we face the threat of super-weeds benefiting more than the crops do from pest resistance.

Yield and Vulnerability. In 1848, the Irish paid a terrible price for relying upon a single high-yield crop (p.82). We seem to have forgotten the lesson. The pursuit of maximum yields leads to over-reliance upon "miracle" crops. They are introduced as soon as they display high yields, long before there has been enough experience to learn how vulnerable they are to pests and disease. The seed industry relies upon its plant breeding techniques to stay ahead of such problems as they arise. This is putting too much confidence in an uncertain gamble.

The dilemma is encapsulated in a recent report from the Philippines:

> LOS BANOS, Laguna, Philippines, August 17, 2000 (ENS) Rice farmers in the Philippines are apprehensive about a plan by the International Rice Research Institute, the world's largest rice research agency, to field test the controversial genetically modified bacterial blight rice, BB-rice.
>
> The farmers are afraid that entry of genetically modified rice into the Philippines will further deplete traditional rice varieties that are sustainable. They also fear that it will mark the beginning of the monopoly and control of rice seeds by multinational companies. . . .
>
> Farmer Tata Gonying Velasco says the use of International Rice Research Institute varieties has not only eroded the diversity of rice the farmers have nurtured for years, it has also wiped out much of farmers' history as "stewards of seeds." . . .
>
> Even Dr. Pamela Ronald who holds the gene's patent . . . acknowledges the problem of blight resistance. "Eight existing bacterial blight isolates can overcome XA21 (the new gene). It is a likely possibility that if XA21 is overcome by the resistant bacterial

blight strains, then an epidemic of unknown proportions can occur," she said. . . .

But Duncan MacIntosh, information officer for the International Rice Research Institute, disputes and brushes off the farmers' claims. . . . (he) maintains that BB-rice is needed because of the world food crisis. "To ensure food security and to continue the advancement against poverty in rice consuming countries of the world, farmers will have to produce 40 to 50 percent more rice to meet the consumer demand in 2025." . . . (but)

"Patents on seeds illustrate the extent to which transnational companies want to establish monopolies on life, maximize profit and dominate the world," farmer Leopoldo Guilaran said. He belongs to MASIPAG, a network of scientists and farmers promoting sustainable agriculture in the Philippines.

"A patent on seed is a patent on freedom. If you have to pay for patented seeds, its like being forced to purchase your own freedom," said Memong Patayan, another MASIPAG farmer. MASIPAG recommends six cultural management practices to control bacterial blight instead of planting BB-rice. These include low use of nitrogen fertilizer, adequate irrigation and drainage, seed-banking of blight resistant plants, and maintenance of crop diversity as well as appropriate transplanting and proper disposal of infected plants. . . .

. . . bacterial blight, a water borne disease aggravated by the use of heavy nitrogen fertilizer, was made worse by the introduction of International Rice Research Institute rice varieties, especially the IR 8 (the so-called "miracle rice") in the mid-1960s.[6]

That about says it. We tamper with the natural systems, then we try to correct the problems we have caused, and we walk deeper and deeper into a bog. The pursuit of high yields led to manipulated rice strains that required heavy nitrogen inputs, which in turn promoted blight. The "miracle" seeds, meanwhile, had led to the abandonment of traditional blight-resistant rice varieties. Now, to correct the mistake, a new genetically manipulated rice variety is proposed, and even the geneticist who discovered the gene says the consequences are uncertain. The Rice Institute defends its program on the basis of the need to increase rice production. Opponents offer a balanced program to deal with the blight, but it would mean using less fertilizer and consequently getting less production.

> Here again, the justification for the gamble is the need to feed more people. If we didn't have to feed more people, we wouldn't need to take that risk. The single-minded pursuit of high yields is a dangerous obsession.

Lower Yields; Better Living. In the first wild rush into modern commercial agriculture, farmers took up monoculture: corn-on-corn or rice-on-rice, with no crop rotation. They relied on chemicals and fertilizer to reach very high yields, but monoculture is great for pests. It serves the corn borer just the lunch it likes, regularly. Crop rotation interrupts its diet. Part of the growth of soybean production in the United States has been a result of farmers' growing wisdom. They have learned to rotate corn with soybeans and thus to reduce their need for commercial fertilizer and pesticides. They also gain protection from market fluctuations or corn blight by producing two crops rather than relying on one.

However, most farmers are not ready to abandon commercial fertilizers or pesticides. With mechanization, they no longer have manure from draft animals. They need to replace the phosphate and potash that is contained in the crop that goes to market. The old style agriculture was labor intensive and would now be costly. Using acreage for pastures or for green manuring with legumes (beyond the marketable soybeans) is not economically competitive, and farmers have to maximize their cash crops to pay their bank debts.

Something seems to have gone wrong. Individual farmers, unless they are heavily capitalized corporations, are in a rat race. The benefit from the high yields goes, not to the farmer, but mostly to those who supply the equipment, the capital, the fertilizer, the pesticides, the hybrid seeds, and those who buy and market the crop—companies like Dow Chemical, Monsanto and Cargill.

Perhaps the commercial farmers should study the Amish in Pennsylvania. Amish farmers are freed by their ethical values from the ferocious pursuit of maximum profit. They don't have to pay off bank debts—or pay perpetual interest—because they raise their own draft horses and make and repair their own wagons and machinery. They don't buy $75,000 tractors or $100,000 combines. They don't pay for commercial fertilizers and pesticides, and they are unworried by the cost of labor because it is their own or their neighbors'. And they live well, in a beautiful countryside of rich farms. Their crop yields may not match Iowa's, but I suspect they are not far off, and their net return is probably higher. It is a pleasant vision of a group that knows how to preserve its independence.

In Europe and China, a comparable recycling agriculture worked for generations for those who were fortunate enough to have a few acres. But as with the Amish, it was labor-intensive.

The catch in this vision of recycling agriculture is that it requires good land, and plenty of it. The problem for the Chinese is that there is not nearly enough land to go around, and it is diminishing, per capita. The industrial world, and now the LDCs, has met the need for food—in a world with a fixed land base—by resorting to ever more expensive and dangerous ways of raising yields. If there was enough land, farmers would not be caught in the rat race.

That brings us to the question: what is the desirable ratio between people and land? Answer: a lot more land per capita than we have now. And the future looks even worse. We need to escape the frantic pursuit of higher yields. And lacking a way to expand the Earth, we must do so by addressing the number of people dependent on it.

Farmland. World arable land has been static since the 1970s, because farmers are using almost all the land that can be used. There is nowhere else to go except onto erosive slopes and less marginal land, or into the forests. Because of population growth, there is now about half as much arable land per capita as in the early '60s.[7] Land is lost to erosion and diverted to urban uses with population growth. To counter the loss and to accommodate their own rising numbers, farmers in the LDCs are burning and cutting forests to convert land to crops, though the land gained is much less suitable for agriculture than the land lost. About 20 percent of tropical forests were lost between 1960 and 1990, and the loss is continuing.[8] In 1997, smoke from forest fires in Indonesia closed airports in other parts of Southeast Asia.

The process is circular and vicious. The loss of forests changes the water cycle. No longer held back by the trees, stream flows become abrupt and erratic. Streams become arroyos, alternating between dry beds and destructive floods. Neither is useful for agriculture, and the floods wash out cropland. Production suffers, intensifying the need to carve more land out of the forests, and the loss of trees contributes to global warming, which in turn contributes to intensified storms and droughts and crop losses—and the need for still more arable land.

That story is hardly new to most readers. I repeat it to make a point: there are synergisms—feedbacks—in our activities that intensify trends. We thus approach crises at accelerating rates. If, on the other hand, we could turn the process around, the synergisms would work to our benefit. As forests returned, the self-reinforcing cycle I described would work in reverse and the pressure on the land and on the farmers would vanish.

I will come back later to the subject of synergisms.

The loss of arable land is most intense in the LDCs that can least afford it, and we cannot even get good measures of the loss. Estimates of arable land in the LDCs are notoriously inexact, and they fail to reflect the estimates of arable land lost. The current official estimate for China is 124 million hectares of arable land. That works out to about 100'x100' per capita (the area of a small suburban lot in the United States). Population growth alone will slice 20 feet off one side of that little plot in the next half century, even if they bring the growth to a halt at 1.5 billion people. And more will be lost to urbanization and erosion.

Compare the Chinese numbers with the United States'; our "plot" is still over 260' x 260' per person, but it has shrunk by nearly half since 1950 because of population growth alone. Urban and industrial sprawl ate up 3.2 million acres of agricultural land each year from 1993 to 1997, compared with 1.4 million acres annually in the preceding decade.[9] Some of that lost land is our best cropland. Total acreage is not at risk as in the third world because we have so much land, but we are losing the best farmland and will replace it with poorer and more erosive land. In places such as Florida and California, much of the lost land was in valuable specialty crops such as grapefruit, lemons, and grapes. We can lose exports and afford imports for a time, but it hurts our economy—particularly as we must spend more and more of our foreign exchange on petroleum (see below).

Crowded countries have lost a much greater share of their cropland. Japan has lost 20 percent since 1961. Western Europe has lost 14 percent.

———————

To sum up the state of agriculture: even without further population growth, we are putting chemicals into the biosphere with unknown and perhaps vast results. We are engaged in an unpredictable battle with pests and weeds, and our choice of weapons may harm us without reducing crop losses. If we look toward a time when the poor eat better, we must anticipate an even more intense pressure on land and water; and "sustainability" is not even theoretically possible unless demand growth stops.

> *A world population of about two billion—one-third of the present population—would not be living off progressively smaller plots of land. To generalize from the example above of pre-modern corn yields, it could raise its food mostly by recycling nutrients rather than unloading fertilizers into the biosphere. It would not need to worry about either the cost of fertilizer or its impact on the environment. It could practice integrated pest management on a scale not now feasible and stop encouraging the mutation of ever more deadly pests. It might even have enough room to retire poor and erosive farmland.*

> *Rising populations would not be crowding out farmland, and farmers would not be burning forests to create more arable land. That alone would benefit agriculture and help to forestall the climate warming in which the human race is now engaged. And arid countries would not be running out of water, as they are now.*

This is a horseback guess, as befits a subject with many unknowns. A study by two leading American scholars concluded on the basis of a much more detailed analysis that the world could support a population somewhat less than two billion.[10]

We are left with the question: why not look at the demand side?

V. IRRIGATION AND WATER

A growing world population has been fed in part by the expansion of irrigation, but irrigation is encountering its limits, because the world is outrunning a limited supply of water.

Irrigation is mankind's major use of water. In arid regions, it accounts for 85 percent or more of all water consumption. Worldwide, it represents 70 percent or more. The world's irrigated acreage has nearly doubled since 1960, in line with population growth, but now we must face the prospect of less irrigation, not more.

 Irrigation results in salinization. Salts build up in the soil if it cannot be flushed regularly, until crops cannot grow in it. This is a problem in natural basins, or where drainage is poor, or where water is too scarce to use it for flushing out the salts. Some irrigation will be abandoned simply because it is self-terminating.

The competition for water is sharpening, driven by population growth and its rising demand for water and food. In dry regions, rivers from the Yellow River to the Rio Grande are literally drying up in the summer. The growing competition is a clear warning to those who hope to feed a more crowded world. The "green revolution" demands more water (and fertilizer) than the crops it replaced.

Estimates have been made of the rate at which groundwater supplies are being depleted, but the data are sparse. From anecdotal evidence, it appears that water tables are falling in much of the arid world, including the United States' southwestern high plains, but oddly enough there does not seem to be an up-to-date systematic inventory of where the water tables are falling, worldwide or even in the United States. One indicator of the stress, however, is that the use of water in the United States has been steady since the 1980s, despite population growth, and per capita withdrawals declined nearly 5 percent in the '90s.[11] Much of this "saving" probably results from the reduced irrigation in the Ogallala Aquifer in the southern Great Plains, as a falling water table has made irrigation unprofitable for some farmers.

Irrigation can be made more efficient, but it is an expensive operation with a one-time gain. And if one saves water by putting it in pipes from the source to the field, it leads to desertification, because the incidental "loss" of water had supplied the moisture for wetlands and gallery forests that supported other species and softened the land and made it tolerable. We are overusing water resources and diminishing their availability for the rest of nature. The first to suffer are the plants and animals that depend upon natural stream flows.

Some irrigation will be given up when, as in the Ogallala, the costs of sinking water tables and rising energy prices outweigh the prospective increase in yields.

> *Again, our problems are on the demand side. Eliminate the requirement for more food production, and the competition for irrigation water eases, there is more available for flushing salts out of the remaining irrigated fields, and more can be left for other species and other uses. Reduce the population and the need for food, and arid countries will be able to accommodate the loss of production as salinization drives out agriculture in natural undrained sinks. They will also be in a position to accommodate greater heat and aridity as global warming proceeds.*

Fresh Water. Irrigation is a subset of the water issue. The growing non-agricultural demand for water threatens irrigation. Cities, industry, residential users, even golf courses outbid agriculture for water. When we most need the food, irrigation water will be diverted to drinking water and industrial supplies. This is already happening in the American west and in China. As a student observed of the American Southwest, it is "rapidly becoming a series of urban archipelagos . . . arrayed across a mostly arid landscape." Irrigation is most needed in arid areas, and it is precisely in those areas that population growth is intensifying the competition for water.

Count this as another feedback loop, as different sectors of growing economic activity compete for the same resources.

The Stockholm Environmental Institute in 1997 assessed world freshwater resources for the United Nations.[12] It is the nearest thing to an official overall appraisal. It reported that water use increased more than twice as much as population growth did in the 20th century, primarily because of increased irrigation and industrial use. About one-third of the world's population already suffers "moderate to high water stress" because of population growth, and the proportion is expected to rise to two-thirds by 2025. At least one-fifth of the world population does not have access to safe drinking water. Half the people in the LDCs suffer from water and food-related diseases. Human contamination threatens not only fresh water supplies but also the health of the oceans. Wildlife species are affected, and the withdrawal of water for human needs is affecting water-dependent environmental systems. The report blames population growth as the first of the "driving forces" causing these changes.

The authors said that the report's conclusions are, if anything, optimistic since they did not attempt to quantify the impacts of global warming on water supplies.

They found that efforts to deal with the situation have not kept up with the deterioration. Economic planners have not sufficiently recognized what water shortages will do to economic growth and especially food production in coming decades. The report observed that about 300 major river basins and many groundwater aquifers cross national boundaries; it took note of the political tensions generated by increasing water scarcity. And it observed that countries with insufficient water to grow their own food will "need access to food grown in water rich regions." It doesn't say how they will pay for it.

A powerful report, but it failed to say that, if population growth is the driver, the solution must include bringing the demand side under control. Other solutions are expensive; they are stopgaps and generate their own problems.

By one estimate, humankind is already using 54 percent of "accessible runoff" (taking account of regional disparities in water supplies). It will need much more to provide for an expanding population.[13] If rivers are drying up and groundwater tables are falling, where will it come from, on a finite Earth? Conservation and recycling can only take us so far.

The answer is that it will be pumped from farther and farther afield—when there is water available somewhere and its owners are willing to part with it. That is hardly a reliable expectation. Canada, which has the most water per capita of any nation, has already taken steps to insure that it is not pumped south to the United States. There are very few areas with a massive surplus and the willingness to part with it.

Then the answer becomes desalinization. For coastal cities, it is a possible solution, but an expensive one. Los Angeles and the Tampa area in Florida are already building desalinization plants to meet part of their growing needs. However, desalination is too expensive for irrigation, at least until food has become very, very expensive. And it becomes progressively less realistic for cities and industry further from salt-water and higher above sea level.

Desalinization contributes to a vicious spiral because it is energy intensive. Most energy, as we shall see, generates carbon emissions and forces climate warming—which in turn forces more demand for water—which then helps to drive the demand for energy and its price upward, making the water progressively more expensive.

As I write this paper, the Food and Agriculture Organization (FAO) is warning of the likelihood of massive starvation in a broad crescent stretching from Afghanistan through Africa. The FAO calls it a sustained drought. There has indeed been a drought. But the effects of drought are magnified when even in good times there is not enough water to go around. And such droughts are precisely the sort of consequence that global warming is expected to produce (see Climate below.)

> *Can we even imagine how much less tense life would be, and how much less deadly droughts would be, if particularly in arid areas there were one-third the population and therefore three times as much water per capita as now, coupled with modern capabilities to manage it?*

People still get some meat from the range, and most of the fish catch is wild rather than raised, but these are limited and threatened sources of food.

Meat. Most meat is raised on grain and hay. The grain is competitive with direct human grain consumption, and the hay competes with other crops for land. Meat is thus a derivative of basic food production, and the tightening food supply, in Figure 1, affects meat supply, too. Grazing animals, however, provide meat that does not compete for grain.

There is more than twice as much rangeland (permanent pasture) as there is cropland, but the range is not an important potential source of food. Only 5 percent of human meat consumption comes from goats and sheep (a rough proxy for range animals.) Those lands are usually sub-marginal for crop production. If they weren't, they would have been used for crops. In the arid less-developed countries, herds of goats and sheep are the scourge of the land because herdsmen chronically overgraze the range in order to feed growing populations. The range would be better off if most nomads could be settled in agriculture (which is being tried in some countries), but there is very little space available for settlement. The western United States raises about 41 percent of the nation's beef from range cattle (though most are fattened on grain). Less than half the rangeland is in "good" condition or better, and its condition is evidence that the number of range cattle should be reduced in everybody's interest, including the ranchers'.

Rangelands are by definition fragile lands, and global warming (see below) is expected to bear heavily on just those zones that are presently given over to rangeland. It will generate higher temperatures, more aridity, and spreading deserts.

We cannot expect pastoral lands, worldwide, to maintain their present level of meat production, to say nothing of helping to feed a growing population.

Fishery and Aquaculture. We don't raise most of the fish we consume; we hunt them. The annual world fish catch in the early 1950s was about 20 million tons, most of it from salt water. To feed a hungry world, the marine catch nearly quadrupled to around 70 million tons in the 1980s—where it has stalled. We have fished the more prized stocks out, one by one. Fishing isn't even cost-efficient. Major fishing nations subsidize their fishermen to keep them employed, thus subsidizing the destruction of a resource and a means of livelihood. It is hard to imagine a more shortsighted policy. With continued overfishing, the question is whether the catch will stay that high.

To make up the gap, nations (particularly China) have turned to aquaculture, which now produces over 20 million tons a year. But there is a fundamental difference: traditional fishery adds a source of protein to that which can be obtained from the land. Aquaculture is a form of animal husbandry, and a very messy one; it competes with livestock and with direct human consumption for grain, and it often competes with grain for land and water. It promotes epidemics among the fish (this is a major problem right now in the shrimp ponds of Southeast Asia). Saltwater pens are massive sources of pollution, and the diseases that originate in the pens spread to the wild stocks. We thus subsidize the destruction of ocean fisheries and promote aquaculture that causes diseases in fish and, perhaps, eventually in those who eat them.

Certain limited forms of aquaculture have long provided a useful source of protein and seem to be benign, such as tilapia rearing in flooded rice paddies, but intensive aquaculture is an environmentally questionable enterprise, like so many other efforts to force natural systems beyond their normal limits and their natural productivity.

If aquaculture is dependent on grain production, what can we expect of ocean fishery as an independent source of protein? The old cliché was that the oceans could support a sustained catch of up to 100 million tons.

As we have seen, that was too optimistic. The question is now whether we can sustain the present catch of 70 million tons in the face of mankind's multiple assault on the marine environment. Consider what we are doing to it:

- The breeding grounds for ocean fish are heavily concentrated in bays and estuaries, which are suffering from eutrophication driven by agriculture and sewage outflows and from multiple industrial pollutants. I have cited the plight of the Chesapeake and the "dead zone" off the Mississippi River estuary.

- Anadromous fish, principally salmon, are disappearing stock by stock, because of dammed rivers, muddied breeding shoals and pollution.

- Human activity is affecting the sea in multiple ways that we barely understand. So far, the impact has been most noticeable on coral reefs and marine mammals and perhaps on the plankton at the bottom of the pelagic food chain. We do not know the tolerance levels of different fish for our environmental insults.

Most of those environmental changes originate on land. The plankton are suffering from increased ultraviolet radiation, a result of human releases of chlorofluorocarbons (CFCs) and other compounds into the stratosphere and the resultant thinning of stratospheric ozone. If the plankton decline, much of the life of the sea will go with them.

Corals are dying and "bleaching" as a result of warming oceans and perhaps of elevated CO^2 from the atmosphere as a result of global warming. A worldwide warming of ocean waters since the 1950s has recently been documented, which tends to confirm the upper projections of global warming.[14] We don't know what that will do to ocean currents and fish stocks as their environment changes.

Nitrates, sulfates and sulfites and other chemicals are being flushed out of the estuaries and washed out of the atmosphere into the open ocean. Poisonous algal "blooms", probably the result of nutrient-laden pollution, have grown more common and caused fish kills in open water.

Our oil-centered civilization is loading hydrocarbons—petroleum products—into the sea. Oil spills from ocean tankers get a lot of attention, but they are just 5 percent of the problem. Most of the oil that enters the oceans is from mundane human activities like changing the oil in our cars and pouring the used oil into the gutter. Routine pumping and cleaning of ships' bilges accounts for 19 percent. Altogether, human discharges account for 91 percent of the petroleum products entering the oceans. Natural seepage accounts for 9 percent.[15]

This catalogue of threats illustrates the ways in which our activities interact and affect our surroundings, and our own interests, in widening circles.

In the face of these assaults, the health of the oceans may not sustain the current 70 million tons of annual marine catch. Let us hope that a return to a smaller catch—perhaps 50 million tons—might be sustainable.

If world population were two billion, one-third its present size, 50 million tons of marine fish would mean half again as much, per capita, as the present take from all fishery, including aquaculture, without running down the stocks. We would not be putting nearly so many pollutants into the sea because we would be using less fertilizer, fewer chemicals, and less energy, and this would mitigate our impact on the ocean. If the 50 million-ton catch is unsustainable, perhaps that suggests an even smaller population would be desirable.

The ten hottest years on record have occurred since 1983, and seven of them have occurred since 1990 despite the cooling effect of airborne ash from the 1991 eruption of the Philippine volcano Pinatubo.[16] Sea levels rose six inches in the 20th century, simply as a result of the expansion caused by ocean warming.[17] Glaciers are melting, the edges are crumbling off the Antarctic ice cap, and in the Arctic the average sea ice thickness has declined 40 percent since the late 1950s, to 4.8'. Snow cover at high latitudes has declined about 10 percent since the 1960s,[18] which reduces Earth's reflectivity and therefore reinforces the warming trend.

Science is finding that we live in a much less stable world than we had assumed. The last century or two have been very kind to human needs, but the study of Greenland ice cores, worldwide sediments and coral reefs has discovered climate shifts much more sudden that we imagined even a decade ago. Sea level has risen some 150 meters (about 500 feet) since the last glacial era, and in one period it rose 16 meters (over 50 feet) in 300 years.[19] There is ice enough left to raise sea level another 300 feet or so if it should all melt, and it may melt faster than we had imagined.

Recently, the National Climate Data Center reports that monthly temperatures in the United States from June 1999 to May 2000 (the latest record as of this writing) have all been the warmest on record. The increase in temperatures could mean more disastrous weather "including droughts, floods and hurricanes," for this country. The Federal Emergency Management Agency Director says, "severe weather disasters in the three years from 1997 through 1999 cost the federal government 337 percent more than during the three years from 1989 through 1991.[20]

The International Panel on Climate Change (IPCC) is the recognized scientific consensus on climate change. In 1995, it predicted a "most likely" warming of 2°C by 2100, with more to follow. And it has described the likely effects: wide swings of weather, more storms, floods, and droughts; rising sea levels (20" or more in the next century); higher temperatures and increased aridity in the tropics, which are already suffering from water shortage and anticipating worse to come. Climate zones and forests will be massively displaced and reduced, and many forested areas will become scrubland. There will be "major adverse effects" on freshwater supplies, fisheries, and biodiversity. The negative effects will be most intense in the tropics, where populations are already the most vulnerable.[21]

The IPCC did not draw conclusions as to the overall impact on agriculture because the authors were not in agreement as to whether the disruption of climate and soil zones would be balanced by the contribution of higher levels of carbon dioxide to plant growth. Subsequent studies have predicted a highly negative net impact on food output in the tropics and semi-tropics from increasing aridity and shifts of climate zones, but more food production at high latitudes because of longer growing seasons. As to the United States, opinion remains divided, with governmental analyses more optimistic than most academic ones. (This probably reflects the ingrained optimism of the Department of Agriculture.)

We are indeed in a warming trend. It is serious, and we have no assurance that it is gradual or brief.

A substantial portion of humanity lives in coastal situations already under threat from hurricanes made increasingly violent by global warming. Bangladesh is the extreme example, where millions of people live on an exposed low delta, and hundreds of thousands die when a typhoon strikes. Hundreds of millions of people worldwide would be threatened even by a rise of a meter or two (3.3–6.6 feet) in sea level. Where would people from the lowlands go in this crowded world if low coasts become unlivable?

A smaller population would have some margin to adapt or to move elsewhere. As a matter of precaution, communities should provide themselves wider margins to adjust to such changes. Too many people are living too close to the edge.

The energy industry and a few apologists have mounted a rearguard action, arguing that the warming, if it is real, is a product of natural climate cycles. There are certainly natural cycles, and lingering uncertainties as to just what they are and how they relate to anthropogenic warming. There are uncertainties about the exact role of the oceans and microbial action, and about how air pollution affects climate. What is still uncertain, however, is less important than the growing certainty that human activity is the cause or a major cause of the current global warming. The models of the theoretical human impact now track very closely the actual changes that have been happening in recent decades, and recent studies have tended to push the projection of climate warming higher—perhaps 3°C–6°C (5°–10°F) in this century in the United States.[22]

Anthropogenic climate warming results mostly from

- Commercial energy carbon releases (mainly in the industrial and rapidly industrializing countries),
- Deforestation (mainly in the less developed countries—see above), and
- other greenhouse gases, notably methane.

Atmospheric carbon dioxide has risen from 280 ppm (parts per million) before the industrial revolution to 363 ppm now. It amazes me how casually the human race is tinkering with the very air it breathes.

The IPCC in 1994 estimated that it would require a 50 to 70 percent reduction in carbon emissions, and a 50 percent reduction in net emissions of nitrous oxides from forest destruction to stabilize the climatic effects at their present level, to say nothing of turning the human impact back to neutral. (Look again at those numbers: a 50 to 70 percent reduction.) Subsequent research has confirmed that estimate.

The Kyoto Convention in 1997 was an effort to address the problem. It came up, finally, with a very modest proposal for an average 5 percent reduction in emissions by the industrial countries by 2008–2012, compared with 1990. It didn't ask for a reduction by the less developed countries, because they claimed the right to "catch up" in per capita emissions. It was a pathetic response to the size of the problem, but it was shaped by political realities and by the unspoken awareness that carbon is a byproduct of fossil energy, that energy is at the center of modern industrial economies, and to tamper with energy production is to threaten those economies.

What has happened to the Convention? Substantially nothing except more meetings. Only a handful of small less-developed countries have ratified the agreement. The world emissions of carbon dioxide have already gone up more than 6 percent since 1990. Forest destruction in the less-developed countries has accelerated.

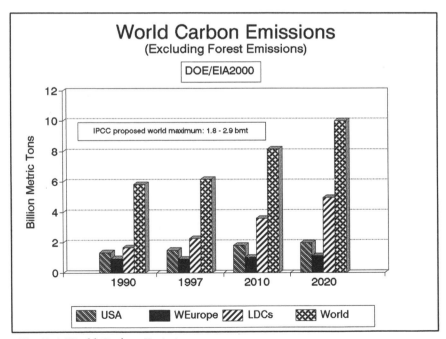

Fig. 7–1 World Carbon Emissions

In 1993, the United States adopted a Climate Change Action Plan. It called for emissions to stay at the 1990 level. It never got off the ground. Our carbon emissions in 1998 were 1.5 billion tons, 15 percent higher than in 1990. By 2020, emissions are expected to be 47 percent higher than in 1990. Why? Mostly, it's because our population will have risen by 31 percent.

Western Europe has done much better, but not well enough. Its emissions actually declined from 1990–1997, but they are expected to rise by 17 percent from 1990 to 2020. Its population is stationary during the period, so population does not drive pollution. Western Europe also reminds us that the United States could be using its energy much more efficiently. It generates just 60 percent as much carbon per capita as we do, partly because it keeps energy prices high and provides an incentive to conserve.

The LDCs' carbon emissions from energy use are much smaller per capita—30 percent of the Western European level—but because of their sheer population numbers they emit nearly as much carbon. They are expected to pass the industrial world by 2010. About 80 percent of the total 1990–2020 growth in worldwide emissions is expected to occur in the LDCs. Their population, and some of their economies, are growing fast, and they rely much more on dirty coal for energy than do the industrial countries.

Overall, the world is expected to emit 72 percent more carbon in 2020 than in 1990. We need a 50–75 percent **decrease**; instead we get a 72 percent **increase** within a generation. (These projections are from the DOE/EIA/IEO2000 "reference" case, basically a continuation of present policies, which the Energy Information Administration considers the most likely course, given the absence of substantial progress to date.[23])

The overwhelming lesson of our experience with climate is that we are not even in the ballpark. If we are to have any prospect of ameliorating the human impact, our only real hope is to move away from fossil energy and to turn world population growth around. Since present growth is largely in the LDCs, such a turnaround would also save tropical forests and reduce their global warming effect. Even with remarkable determination, we couldn't make those changes fast enough to prevent continued anthropogenic climate warming with all its consequences. But the efforts are still worthwhile, because they point toward an eventual solution. They start to address the question, how much worse are we willing to let things get?

The industrial world alone cannot solve the problem. The great growth engine is the combination of population and economic growth in the LDCs. Only with their determined cooperation is there any prospect of eventually bringing our climate experiment under control. One ray of hope is that the Chinese are beginning to admit it; they have signed agreements with South Korea and Japan (February 2000) and with the United States (May 2000) to cooperate in joint efforts to address air and water pollution and climate change.

> *It is a sobering thought that, if the world had stopped population growth by 1960—when it was half the present level—we would now be a long way toward the "50 percent to 70 percent reduction" called for by the IPCC, even with our present wasteful practices. If it had stopped at two billion, we would not have a problem.*

Fossil energy, along with agriculture, is the origin of most of our problems with climate change, soil, water and air pollution. We are annually pumping petroleum and gas and digging up coal that had been sequestered in the lithosphere over millions of years, and putting them back into the biosphere. This is a fundamental alteration of the carbon, nitrogen, sulphur, and mercury balance at which the Earth's biosphere had arrived. Nature recycles those things; we are injecting them into the system. None of that addition is "natural". The question is, how long will this go on, and at what level?

Fossil energy is the environmental villain, but it won't last forever, and technology already offers the alternative of benign—but expensive—alternatives. In this one area, technology, coupled with a rethinking of the role of the internal combustion engine, offers a real prospect of making a substantial reduction in the environmental damage we are now doing. There is, in other words, a trade-off: how much improvement we can get through investment and technological fixes vs. how much population reduction we need. The trade-off is not symmetrical. The word "investment" is critical, as is the resolve to make it. Much of the technological reform is costly and disruptive, while a gradual population decline actually saves money on capital investment and can be done with little disruption.

Worldwide consumption of commercial energy rose 10 percent from 1990 to 1997, despite the general worldwide economic recession of the mid-1990s. It is projected to rise another 60 percent by 2020. Fossil fuels—the culprits in global warming and atmospheric pollution—presently provide 84 percent of that energy, and the proportion is actually expected to rise to 89 percent by 2020, because nuclear power is expected to play a smaller role by then. Renewable energy (mostly hydroelectric power) is holding steady at 8 percent of the total supply.

For the United States, the energy growth from 1990 to 1997 was 12 percent and the anticipated growth by 2020 will be another 28 percent. Western Europe is expected to do better, as the above discussion of carbon emissions suggested. Its energy use for the whole period 1990–2020 is expected to rise only 9 percent.

The real drivers (again in line with the carbon emission projections) are the LDCs. Their total energy use is expected to be more than three times as high in 2020 as in 1990; China's energy use will be 3.6 times as high.

Resources of hydrocarbons are being depleted, but not so fast as to spare us the prospect of continuing climate warming and environmental damage for generations ahead.

Oil. The world's resources, proven and unproven, are now estimated at 2.189 trillion barrels.[24] The estimate has been rising because of new optimism about technology and the ability to pump oil in the deep ocean. The estimate works out to sixty plus years of consumption, assuming demand continues to grow. That is not very long, but of course oil won't simply run out then. It will get more and more expensive. Users will look to other energy sources, and oil will be pumped only for high-value uses like chemical feedstock.

The United States has already pumped out about 70 percent of the oil we started with. About 69 billion barrels remain. How much is that? Americans consume seven billion barrels a year, and the Energy Information Administration expects consumption to rise 1.3 percent per year through 2020. At that rate, there are nine years' consumption left. Or, more practically: the United States imports 58 percent of the crude oil it consumes, and that is expected to rise to 69 percent by 2010. That extends the resource, but the nation had better be ready to pay for a lot more imported oil, very soon—at prices that have already risen sharply— or do with less.

A growing population will make the transition from petroleum more abrupt, as it consumes more and more of the grain it has been exporting to earn foreign exchange for oil imports.

The United States estimate assumes a price of $30 per barrel—about where it is at the moment. From there on up the supply is highly inelastic and you don't get much more oil for higher prices. There will be a move to gas and coal. And at prices above $30, benign alternative sources such as wind and solar energy will become competitive for more and more uses.

Natural Gas. Gas is the fastest growing fuel, because it is cheap, relatively clean (compared especially to coal) and convenient. World consumption is expected to rise 2.7 percent a year through 2020. At that rate, known worldwide reserves will last 37 years—but that figure may double as anticipated discoveries of new gas resources are confirmed. Roughly speaking, remaining world gas resources are about equal to oil resources. As with petroleum, estimates of total resources have been rising, but the world is coming to the end of both energy resources in this century, and some countries far earlier than that. Gas is not as concentrated as oil, but most of it is in the Middle East and the former Soviet Union countries.

North American proven reserves will last about a decade, but estimates of unproven gas resources vary widely, depending on assumptions about price and technology. There may be several decades' supply. The United States is unique in that we have already used perhaps half the original resources. That circumstance argues against continuing to allow our energy demand to grow.

Coal is the sleeper. It presently constitutes 24 percent of world fossil energy consumption; its use is going up, but its share of total energy consumption is expected to decline slightly. It is dirty and unpopular, and it is the most polluting fossil fuel, but it is a cheap fuel for generating electricity. Estimated resources will last well into the 22nd century, even if the consumption rate goes up. Our industrialists may rejoice, and environmentalists lament, that the United States has the world's largest proven reserves, 25 percent of the total. Another 56 percent is concentrated in the countries of the former USSR, China, Australia, India, Germany and South Africa, in that order.

Coal can be made much cleaner to use if it is gasified. Known gasification technologies can bring the pollution way down—and the cost way up. At the experimental gasification plant at Cool Water, California, most of the polluting emissions, except carbon dioxide, were sequestered and some were resold. It has been shut down for years. I was told that, even with the capital investment in place, the plant would be competitive only if petroleum prices rose to $40 per barrel. That figure would probably be higher now.

That price is not necessarily bad news. At such a base price for clean energy, more benign sources become more competitive. However, it is very hard to sell governments (particularly in the third world) on expensive gasification technology, even though their cities are gagging on air pollution. They have been unwilling even to pay for less ambitious clean-up technologies. China and India are expected to account for 97 percent of the increase in coal use by 2020—and they are not even installing scrubbers to take out the sulfur. Only 3 percent of China's coal power plants have scrubbers.

One or another fossil fuel enthusiast regularly turns up with proposals to utilize tar sands or methane sequestered in the coastal slopes of oceans to extend the fossil fuel era. Those proposals rest on very shaky assumptions of feasibility, and scientists have warned that the effort to get at the dispersed methane in the oceans could trigger mudslides and a disastrous release of methane (a potent greenhouse gas) into the atmosphere. Our environmental experience suggests it would be wiser to phase fossil fuels out rather than trying to extend them.

Nuclear power has most of the problems one can think of. It is expensive and terribly dangerous. We cannot manage its wastes. Like fossil fuels, it is a transitional source of energy because of the limits of available uranium—unless it is processed for reuse in ways that invite nuclear weapon proliferation and diversion to terrorists or gangsters.

But it doesn't emit carbon dioxide.

DOE/EIA expects the retirement of nuclear plants in the industrial countries to outweigh the construction of new ones in the LDCs, and it predicts a decline of nuclear power as a fraction of total energy from 7 percent now to 3 percent in 2020. Things may or may not work out that way. In Europe, France relies on nuclear energy for most of its electricity; Britain is heading that way. Germany and Sweden, on the other hand, are phasing nuclear power out because of its environmental dangers. (Germany is actually producing 1 percent of its energy with wind power.) There is considerable tension within the European Union about which way to go. A recent report (by a British consulting firm to the European Commission) touted nuclear energy as the solution to fossil fuel emissions and called for the construction of 85 nuclear power plants.[25] Russia, too, is considering a proposal for 23 new nuclear plants, despite memories of Chernobyl. And Spain is considering going nuclear. It is a devil's choice, forced upon them by the demand for more energy and the prospective lack of fossil fuels.

Renewables. Hydroelectricity provides 6 percent of present world energy, but it faces a static future. The best sites have been taken. The remaining ones in the crowded third world exact a tremendous price in the loss of farmland and the displacement of people.

Biomass (burning wood and plant fiber, as we used to do, or converting it to ethanol) will have a limited role because it competes for land needed to produce food, wood and cellulose.

The good news lies in the environmentally benign "renewables", particularly wind and, to a lesser degree, direct solar power. Estimates of their cost vary with the enthusiasm of the estimator and with the intended use. Wind power is becoming nearly competitive with fossil fuels in some locations, for supplemental power. The Wind Power Association claims it can be delivered to utilities for three to six cents per kilowatt/hour (KWH).[26] The leading American windpower company suggests a range of three to five cents, very much dependent on the location and on the nature and level of governmental subsidies and inducements. (There is a U.S. federal subsidy presently set at 1.7 cents per KWH.) Since fossil power delivered to the grid costs approximately three cents per KWH, wind power is right at the edge of being economically competitive. If fossil fuels were priced at a level compensating for their environmental damage—perhaps an impossible calculation—windpower would probably be more than competitive now.[27]

Solar power is farther off, except for isolated locations and uses requiring very limited amounts of power. The utility companies say that solar energy costs five times as much as fossil fuels, and this ratio has not changed much in several years.

Both solar and wind power offer the promise of dispersed, small scale power, lower transmission losses, and freedom from the massive blackouts that attend continental scale electric power grids. Unfortunately, windpower requires that the wind blow hard enough (but not too hard), and photovoltaics need sunlight. They are erratic sources, which poses a fundamental problem. So long as they provide a very small fraction of the power in a grid, the price comparisons above remain relevant. If, however, they should have to take over some or the entire task of providing reliable baseline power, they are going to get much more expensive, because of the cost of storing the energy.

Hydrogen. There are several ways of storing this erratic energy supply, none of them very satisfactory. Hydrogen is probably the most promising, as a means of storage and a fuel that can be used directly in fuel cell vehicles and generators. Environmentally, it is the most benign of fuels; it can be obtained from plain water, with oxygen as the only byproduct. Burning it generates only water vapor. The technology is understood. Wind and eventually photovoltaic electricity can provide the power to isolate the hydrogen, probably by electrolysis or maybe even by microbial fermentation or enzymes. The problem is the cost. The present steam process for generating hydrogen is far from competitive with fossil fuels, and electrolysis costs about three times as much again.

Although this may change, the new processes now under intensive study do not yet offer any assurance that they will be cheap.

The fearsome aspect of hydrogen is its volatility. Anybody who remembers pictures of the explosion of the airship Hindenberg is indelibly aware of its dangers. But, after all, we have learned to live with gasoline, which in addition to its environmental penalties is highly explosive.

Conclusion . . . The world, and particularly the United States, has used energy inefficiently because it has been cheap. Now, however, as we move down the road we are on, everything takes more energy: agriculture, water, infrastructure, environmental cleanups, and energy production itself. And the more fossil or nuclear energy, the greater the environmental stress. The United States is particularly vulnerable because of its high demand and the problematical future of our petroleum and gas resources.

Making the energy transition to benign sources is the most immediate contribution that science and technology could make to a sustainable future. With energy, unlike food, we are in a zone of trade-offs rather than absolute limits. The exhaustion of fossil fuels will force us toward cleaner technologies, but because of the abundance of coal, that is an uncertain and distant salvation. The transition itself will be resisted so long as the coal is there, and because benign energy will cost much more. Diffuse and irregular energy, like wind and sunlight, cannot be collected and stored as cheaply as oil or gas coming out of a wellhead. Given the public and industry resistance to more expensive energy, the EIA specialists are probably right in their cynical expectation that fossil energy will not be displaced by a significant shift to benign sources in the foreseeable future—whatever that may mean for the climate.

When it comes, the transition will be an immense, expensive, and technologically challenging undertaking, and rising energy prices themselves will make it more expensive. It is a challenge, not a wall; but the required capital can best be mobilized if energy investments are not com-

peting with investment in infrastructure—the construction and maintenance of roads, cities, schools, factories, housing, and other physical
plant.

> *A smaller population demands less energy, which is help-
> ful during our present fossil fuel dependence. Moreover,
> a declining population would be helpful during the
> energy transition, because it requires much less infra-
> structure investment than a rising or static population.
> The lucky inhabitants could use the best of the existing
> physical plant—and the least polluting power plants and
> factories—and retire the rest.*

The energy transition will lead to some fundamental shifts in economic relationships. The transition will be uneven because of the uneven
distribution of fossil fuels. The long-term gainers and losers will also
shift. The arid tropics and semi-tropics will be energy-rich (as only a few
of them are now) because they can exploit sunlight—even as they
become more water-poor. Windy steppes will be at a premium, and certain concentrated wind sites like mountain passes. Europe and Japan are
already energy-poor and will remain so.

> *The countries with limited potential have a special
> inducement to bring their demand, and their population,
> in line with their limited renewable energy resources.*

There is some reason for satisfaction. Conventional pollution of the air and water have declined somewhat in the industrial world because of the growing awareness of the environment. As to solid wastes, 27 percent of municipal waste is now recycled in the United States, but 116 million tons still go into landfills each year. The European experience suggests that the recycled proportion could be doubled. After that, further gains probably depend on changing our packaging and consumption habits—and on the size of the population. There have been gains in industrial toxic releases, but they still total 3.3 million tons annually. Pesticide residues in food samples have gone down somewhat since the 1970s. They are still found in 34 percent of the samples, but only about 1 percent of the samples are over EPA's permissible levels.[28] I think it is fair to generalize this way: industrial nations have had some success in dealing with the pollution sources recognized early, but they are learning how much more pervasive the problem is than was originally thought.

The less-developed countries do not have even that satisfaction. Pollution is rising to levels that the industrial world never suffered, and there is no end in sight.

The release of minerals and chemicals into "the environment" is worldwide. This is not an external abstraction. Those substances have made their way into plants and animals, all of us, around the planet, and we don't know the consequences. In this section, I will explore the issue sector by sector.

The Atmosphere. I will start on a high note. In the United States (as in Europe), the battle with air pollution is one of our few real environmental success stories. We have not been able to stop the growth of carbon dioxide emissions, but since 1978, thanks to legislation such as the Clean Air Act of 1970, we have reduced carbon monoxide emissions by 32 percent, sulfur dioxide by 35 percent, fine particulates by 37 percent, lead emissions by 98 percent. The atmosphere has improved roughly in line with those gains. Nitrogen oxides have gone up 11 percent, but that is a lot less than population growth and rising automobile use would have caused without the Act.

If we have won those battles, we have also learned the limits of technical fixes. We have run out of the cheaper gains. Broadly speaking, we have taken most of those gains to their conclusion but we have not yet really grappled with the automobile culture. The question is, where can further improvements come from?

Let us look at five EPA graphs of emissions trends in the past decade.[29]

Sulfur dioxide. The gains were finished by 1984. Economic stagnation led to a slight decline in the early '90s, but prosperity has brought a rising trend since then.

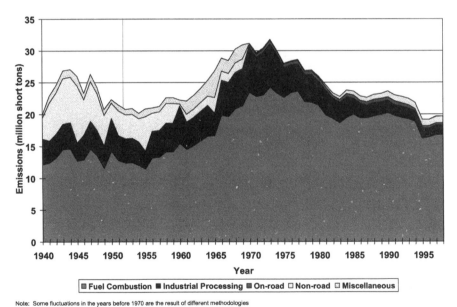

Note: Some fluctuations in the years before 1970 are the result of different methodologies

Fig. 9–1. Trend in Sulfur Dioxide Emissions, 1940 to 1998

Sulfur emissions are almost entirely the product of electricity generation, particularly from coal burning power plants. There are still some old plants, particularly in the Middle West, that are heavy emitters and are currently the targets of a lawsuit filed by EPA and the Eastern downwind states. This gives us room for some further small gains, but the solution will not come until coal gasification and alternative energy are forced upon us.

Nitrogen oxides. The twin culprits here are energy generation and the automobile. Technical fixes are harder to come by than with sulfur dioxide, and our national love affair with the automobile has dampened our legislators' enthusiasm for doing anything serious.

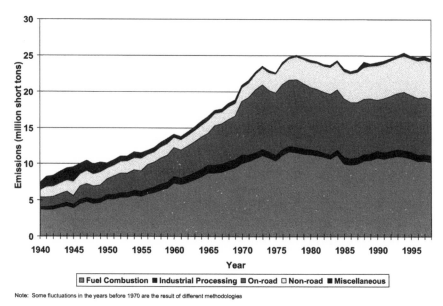

Note: Some fluctuations in the years before 1970 are the result of different methodologies

Fig. 9–2. Trend in Nitrogen Oxide Emissions, 1940 to 1998

Average mileage per gallon has been declining since 1988. It peaked at 25.9 mpg then; it is down to 23.8 mpg now.[30] The graph tells it all. Progress has stagnated because of consumers' new passion for sports utility vehicles (SUVs) and Congress' unwillingness to discourage it.

> *If this reflects the national level of commitment to environmentally benign behavior, we need a much lower U.S. population to contain the consequences of our living habits.*

Much the same story can be said of *fine particulates*, which the EPA began to log only a decade ago when it became clear that fine particulates are more serious threats to health than soot. We have not progressed since then.

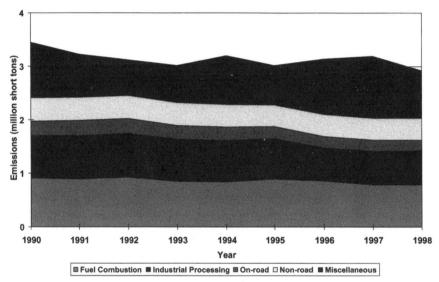

Fig. 9–3. Trend in Directly Emitted Fine Particle Matter

Ozone emissions have flattened since 1988, and the effect of ozone on children, asthmatics, and bronchial disease sufferers has become a hot new issue.

Figure 9–4 shows that we have quite a way to go. The EPA reports that there are 107 million Americans living in counties with air pollutant concentrations above the national air quality standards, mostly because of ozone. The American Lung Association (ALA), drawing on the same data, says "More than 132 million Americans live in areas with dangerous levels of smog... While emissions of some air pollutants have gone down, and the nation's overall air quality has improved over the past 30

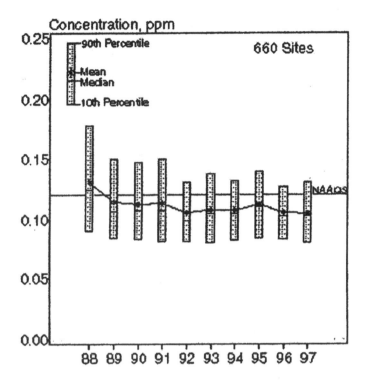

*Fig. 9–4. Trend in Annual Second-Highest Daily Maximum 1-hour O^2
Concentrations, 1988 to 1997*

years, much of that progress has been in eliminating obvious pollution
and sources. Many of the less visible pollutants, such as ozone, have been
reduced far less, and as understanding of the health effects of air pollution has advanced, it has become clear that much of the nation still faces
major air pollution problems."[31]

Here is one final graph; it shows *lead* emissions. We made spectacular
gains in the '70s and '80s by taking lead out of gasoline and paints, but
we have reached a plateau.

Not very high, perhaps, but it is cumulative and does not include the
lead that is leaching into groundwater from mining tailings, dumps, and
other sites all over the country (see below). Lead is getting into the biosphere at a rate unknown before the industrial revolution. We tend to
score our environmental successes like a ball game, but air pollution is

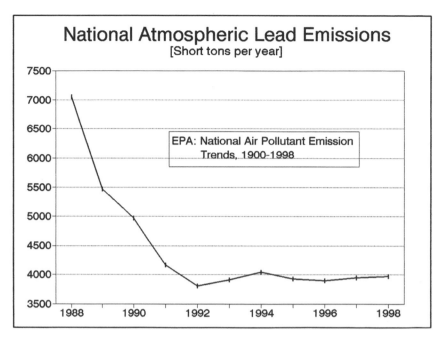

Fig. 9–5. National Atmospheric Lead Emissions

just one ball game. What happens to the lead when it leaves the air? What is the cumulative impact? We don't know how to answer those questions, because our scientific methods have trouble dealing with such broad issues. (The government of Denmark tried to ban all products containing lead, but the European Union ruled out the proposed regulations because the environmental impact was, it said, insufficiently documented.)

The reader will notice that none of the above graphs deals with rising carbon dioxide levels and global warming. Nor do they cover all the bases. Coal has unpleasant by-products such as mercury. It is a heavy metal that becomes intensely toxic when transformed by microbial action. A recent study tabulated annual releases of 179,000 pounds of mercury from the smokestacks and in the cinder ash of 400 U.S. power plants.[32] The Minimata or "dancing cat disease" outbreak in Japan resulted from mercury poisoning when people ate fish poisoned by trace amounts from a nearby factory. One gram of mercury per year in a 25-acre lake can make the fish unsafe to eat. Even the trout in idyllic remote mountain lakes are now unsafe. Most states in this country have set advisory warnings as to how much freshwater fish can safely be consumed.

I have been discussing the United States. The worldwide problem of air pollution and acid deposition is expected to intensify in coming decades. The major LDCs are emerging into the industrial era, and there is not much evidence that they recognize the severity of the problems they are creating. China and India alone constitute 38 percent of the world's population—twice the size of the present industrial world. As they industrialize, sulphur dioxide emissions in Asia are expected to treble from 1990 to 2010.

There is immense pressure building on the environment as poor nations seek to live the "good life," and the rich demonstrate that they are not inclined to abandon it.

> *In so far as the world cannot or will not pay for expensive technologies to manage pollution, we would be well advised to reduce the population-driven demand that multiplies it.*

The Land. In the air pollution statistics I cited, the popular assumption is that we have disposed of the problem. More accurately, we have slowed the rate at which we make things worse. Moreover, we have often simply transferred the issue to the land and water. Air pollution eventually descends on forests, farmlands, grassland, lakes, and the sea. I have mentioned lead and mercury, but nitrogen saturation is an even more pervasive question. I have discussed the environmental impacts of nitrogen fertilizers, but airborne nitrogen is even more ubiquitous than fertilizer. It leaches forests of nutrients, eutrophies lakes, and reduces the diversity of grasslands. The World Resources Institute says that "While the risks of global warming... are fairly common knowledge today, the dangers of the world's heavy nitrogen habit have gone largely unheralded so far, although this habit may be as pervasive and hard to address as cutting greenhouse gas emissions."[33]

Lakes and forests have not recovered as much from the reduced emissions of pollutants as scientists had expected. The "damage... from acid deposition may be more fundamental and long-lasting than was at first believed."[34] This seems to be a demonstration of scientists' generalized warnings that it may be generations before the consequences of our activities become evident.

Several studies have been undertaken to measure the human impact on the Earth by measuring the human appropriation of the total energy available from photosynthesis or the human disturbance to the land. Those estimates suggest that human activity is affecting something like 40 percent of terrestrial nature. The examples I have been discussing would suggest that such measurements understate our impact; it is universal.

Water and Health. I will deal first with the *poor countries*. Urban populations in the less-developed countries have grown sixfold since 1950, from 304 million to two billion; they are expected to pass four billion by 2030. Those dry numbers do not convey the horror of expanding slums, festering in the breakdown of urban services and the lack of basic necessities like clean water. Some 90 percent of the sewage in those cities go untreated into ditches and watercourses, and much of it is re-used immediately by people with no other option.[35]

Rural populations have doubled, and some well-intended improvements actually promote disease. Irrigation, with its stagnant or slow-moving water, has promoted diseases such as malaria, schistosomiasis, river blindness, dengue fever, encephalitis, and filariasis.[36] By one estimate, 50 percent of the people in less developed countries are suffering at any given time from water and food-related diseases.[37]

> *To argue that those governments could do better, as crowded Europe does, is to miss the point. Their success has been their failure. They have been overwhelmed by numbers and, unlike Europe, continuing population*

*growth wipes out the health gains they made, and which
had made the population growth possible.*

Now let us look at *the industrial world*. In the United States, we have
had less success with water pollution than with air pollution, despite
massive efforts such as interceptor sewers. The proportion of lakes and
rivers in satisfactory condition has stayed fairly constant in recent
decades and is now about 58 percent of the total area sampled. Some
measures of water quality have improved, but the fecal bacteria count, a
key indicator, has risen again.[38] Nitrates and phosphates show no partic-
ular trend, which suggests that the ongoing loading from the land is
going out to sea or being absorbed and perhaps transformed in lake bot-
toms. Something is happening to it, and our lack of knowledge is a bit
disconcerting.

The industrial world treats its drinking water to get rid of the
pathogens, but we are forced more and more to recycle it. The idea of
drinking processed sewage is initially a shock, but we are getting used to
it as we press harder on the supply. Recycling should also remove the
nitrates, to protect our health and the downstream environment, but that
requires expensive tertiary treatment, and only about half the sewage
plants in the United States (measured by capacity) have that capability.
Even some of the tertiary treatments fail to get rid of the nitrates; they
simply move the nitrogen out of the water and onto the land rather than
returning it to the air as an inert gas. Here again, heavy use of a resource
leads to rising costs to deal with the consequences of overuse.
Municipalities have not spent the money to keep up with the damage.

Another nasty problem has just been recognized: the recycling of
drugs. Researchers in Europe, Canada, the United States and Brazil have
found medical drugs in water samples. The human race is addicted to
medicine, and some of the drugs pass through the human body into
sewage water and then into lakes and streams, and then back into drinking water. The drugs include painkillers, various cholesterol regulators,
antiseptics, chemotherapy agents, antibiotics, and hormones. Drug
residues were detected in all 64 drinking-water samples collected in

Berlin. Even tertiary treatment won't get rid of them. It requires another step: activated carbon filters.

Documented ecological impacts include the occurrence of anti-biotic resistant bacteria in rivers (including salmonella in the Rio Grande) and in birds, and sexual disruption of fish exposed to estrogenic chemicals. "Male fish in rivers receiving sewage effluent produce the female egg-yolk protein, vitellogenin, resulting from exposure to estrogenic compounds... in the low part-per-trillion range. The presence of vitellogenin in male fish has been related to widespread intersexuality, the appearance of female characteristics and the progressive disappearance of male characteristics, in the United Kingdom. Intersexuality can be a serious threat to the survival of affected species."[39]

So far, the observation has been limited to fish and birds. Studies of the health effects of drinking other people's recycled drugs are just getting under way. Various changes have been observed in humans, including the increase in feminine characteristics and declining sperm counts among males. They have been attributed to the practice of feeding estrogens and other hormones to livestock. I wonder if we may learn that recycled drugs play a role. A cheerful note.

> *These threats and dangers are imposed even on the industrial world by the effort to overuse our water resources. Why do we insist on punishing ourselves and our fellow creatures like this?*

Chemicals. The problem of chemicals is all-pervasive. Let me quote the Illinois regional director of EPA when he learned that people were using the tailings of an abandoned mine as landfill:

> Springfield, IL, May 8, 2000 (ENS). We want everyone to know this is not clean fill; it is not safe to use, said Skinner. The tailings at the mine, which look similar to limestone, have been analyzed and revealed high levels of lead, arsenic and zinc. Exposure to lead can affect the central nervous system, kidneys and immune system.

Lead exposure is dangerous to young and unborn children, leading to premature births, smaller babies, decreased mental ability, learning difficulties and reduced growth. Arsenic exposure may result in gastrointestinal irritation, with symptoms such as pain, nausea, vomiting and diarrhea. Breathing inorganic arsenic increases the risk of lung cancer, and ingesting it increases the risk of skin cancer and tumors of the bladder, kidney, liver and lung. Breathing large amounts of zinc can cause an illness called metal fume fever. Consuming large amounts of zinc over a short period of time can cause stomach cramps, nausea and vomiting. Consuming zinc for a longer period of time may cause anemia, damage to the pancreas, nervous system effects, and lower the levels of "good" cholesterol in the body. Zinc levels in soil above those needed for maximal plant growth may produce toxic effects on plants.[40]

Agriculture is hardly alone in transferring minerals from the lithosphere to the biosphere. And that report is about just three minerals. Mine tailings send downstream a witches' brew of toxic substances such as thorium, heavy metals, nitrates, and chlorides. The EPA reports that industry released 3.3 million metric tons of toxins in the United States in 1998. Mining and electric power are the biggest culprits, representing almost two thirds of the total.

New chemical compounds add to the brew. The American Chemical Society maintains the worldwide database for chemicals. Through 1999, it had registered over 22 million compounds; twice as many as it had by 1990 and four times as many as by 1980. (Of the 22 million, nearly six million were biosequences registered after 1993; this reflects the enormous growth of the genetic manipulation industry.) Not all of these substances are produced in significant quantities, of course. Perhaps 75,000 of them are commercially traded. Some of them such as fertilizers or industrial sulphuric acid enter the environment in enormous quantities.

We are just learning about the impact of even trace minerals and chemicals on life processes, but we haven't yet put it together. There is no tabulation of the potential health or environmental effects of that incredible myriad of chemicals. The National Academy of Sciences (NAS) in 1984 examined the literature on a tiny sample of commercially traded chemicals and concluded that we have barely begun to test them for their primary health effects. There are even fewer studies of their impact as they move through the environment and are transformed by chemical and microbial action. We do not know how their accumulation will affect the support systems on which we depend, particularly the microbes that have buffered their impact. And, apparently, the state of our knowledge has not advanced much since 1984.

A new scientific study illustrates my concern about what happens when those chemicals are transformed in the environment. Researchers have discovered a previously unknown gas, SF^5CF^3, which sounds like the ultimate nightmare for those trying to address global warming. Molecule for molecule, it is the most powerful greenhouse gas yet discovered—18,000 times more powerful than carbon dioxide. Unlike carbon dioxide, there are no known sinks or natural processes to absorb it, and it may dwell in the atmosphere for 3200 years. The discoverers speculate that it may be the breakdown product of a gas used as an insulator in high voltage electrical equipment, but they don't know. It apparently came into existence only during the past forty years. It presently is found in the atmosphere in almost infinitesimal amounts, but it is increasing 6 percent per year.[41] That growth rate may not be sustained but it would mean a 340-fold increase in this century. The sources of that gas must be discovered and rooted out if there is to be a permanent solution to anthropogenic climate warming. And this may be just one of the surprises our industrious chemical industry has in store for all of us.

Let me move now to a more immediate problem that is better understood. I will quote at length from one particularly dramatic exposition, because it says what I am trying to say, but with much greater authority. It is about the chlorine family, whose members include everything from PVC plastics to dioxin:

> New York, June 7, 2000 (ENS) They are part of a group of chemicals known as organochlorines, formed when chlorine gas produced by the chemical industry comes into contact with organic matter in industrial processes. There are 11,000 organochlorines produced commercially, and thousands more are formed as byproducts. They share the dangerous properties of persistence and stability in the environment, and accumulation in the fatty tissues of animals and humans. Although organochlorines have only been produced in large amounts since 1940, they now blanket the entire planet, reaching from the deep oceans to the high Arctic, from the Mississippi River to the Amazon rainforests.
>
> "Everyone on Earth now eats, drinks and breathes a constantly changing and poorly characterized soup of organochlorines, including dozens of compounds that cause severe health damage at low doses," said Joe Thornton, a biologist at Columbia University's Center for Environmental Research and Conservation.
>
> Thornton has written a new analysis of the global consequences of organochlorines, known as persistent organic pollutants (POPs). "Pandora's Poison: Chlorine, Health and a New Environmental Strategy" presents a compelling body of evidence suggesting that these chemicals have already begun to cause large scale damage to public health, including increasing cancer rates and impaired child development.

Analyses of human fat, mothers' milk, blood, breath, semen and urine demonstrate that everyone—not just those living near major pollution sources—now carries a "body burden" of toxic organochlorines in his or her tissues. At least 190 organochlorines, including dioxins, PCBs and DDT, have been identified in the tissues and fluids of the general population of the U.S. and Canada. Hundreds more are present but have not been chemically characterized.

Organochlorines have been linked to immune system suppression, falling sperm counts and infertility, as well as learning disabilities in children. More than 100 organochlorines cause cancer in laboratory animals or humans. . . . the more you eat, the more you carry. Animals higher up the food chain, such as eagles, wolves and humans, carry the burden of all the organochlorines from the meat they have eaten. In the Great Lakes region of the U.S., dioxin and related compounds have caused epidemic reproductive, developmental and immune system damage in fish, birds and mammals... Polar bears, which eat fish, seals and other heavily contaminated animals, carry some of the world's highest levels of organochlorines in their tissues. "Contamination of polar bear tissues with dioxins and PCBs is so severe, in fact, that the bears' body burdens exceed by a substantial margin the levels that are known to cause reproductive failure, immune suppression and altered brain development in other kinds of mammals," Thornton writes.

Humans are not immune. Dioxin exposure is particularly severe for Arctic peoples, who eat a diet similar to the polar bears. Dioxin levels in the milk of Inuit mothers are two to 10 times higher than in the rest of the U.S. and Canadian populations.

"Organochlorines interfere with the basic machinery with which the body regulates itself," said Thornton. 'They are incompatible with basic physiological functions.' Because organochlorines are so stable in the environment, even banned substances like the pesticide DDT continue to poison the ground and water. Related chemicals, including Dursban, the most widely used pesticide in the U.S., are only now coming under restrictions.

"Organochlorines can't be reduced to a handful of bad actor compounds like DDT," he said . . . "Virtually all organochlorines tested have one or more toxic effects . . . . regulators and legislators should begin treating organochlorines not as individual substances but as single entity. ... Of the thousands of organochlorines in production, only a small fraction has been subject to basic toxicity testing, and complete health hazard information is available for none. Developing the information base to predict the health impacts of each chemical would take centuries, and in the meantime, the public is exposed to a cocktail of untested substances. . . . Even acceptable discharges build up to unacceptable levels." . . . Already, the average body burden of dioxin alone in the U.S. is at or near the range where reproductive, developmental and immunological effects occur in laboratory animals. This newly named carcinogen is produced at some point during the lifecycle of all chlorine-based chemicals—in the production of chlorine gas, the synthesis of all organochlorines, and the combustion of any organochlorine product or waste . . . The levels of dioxin in the environment can only increase, as long as organochlorines are produced,

Thornton warns. "Once we've got them, we've got them, and there's no safe way of disposing of them . . ."[42]

Sympathize with the polar bears, trying to survive out on the thinning ice floes and accumulating toxins. Sympathize with us. The organochlorides are targeted directly at our own species, since we are high on the food chain. If your doctor is telling you to eat more vegetables and less meat, this is another convincing reason to listen.

The EPA has been wrestling for a decade with the risks from dioxins and it has just released parts of a revised assessment for public and scientific review. Thornton timed his news conference to coincide with an announcement by EPA that it has negotiated the phase-out of Dursban with the major producers, but he dismissed such actions as a hopeless effort to address just one of the issues posed by the organochlorine family.

Thornton is not alone. More than 100 prominent physicians, public health professionals, and scientists have appealed to the President "to develop a plan of action, which should include national and international commitments to the long-term goal of the virtual elimination" of the dioxin group. The executive director of Physicians for Social Responsibility said, "The industries flooding our environment with dioxin have denied its dangers while this report has been held up for nine years . . . This reassessment tells the truth they don't want you to hear: dioxin is a dangerous cancer causing chemical that must be phased out . . . "[43] The Director of EPA has called organochlorides a "World War II era" family of chemicals that should be phased out. As with mercury, or lead, or the other pollutants described above, the realization was belated.

Those concerns, and the industry's resistance to hearing them, tell us a good deal about the problems of dealing with the explosive proliferation of chemicals in the past half-century. Chemicals are presumed innocent until proven guilty, and that is not enough for our protection. Both of the quotations above refer to clinical evidence of impairment to child development. Similar citations appear regularly in the literature. We worry about the widespread evidence of learning deficiencies among American children. I wonder whether the problems may have chemical as well as social roots.

Prudence would suggest that we delay the introduction of chemicals until we understand them well enough to have some confidence that they are harmless. What we are learning tells us to abandon our headlong flight into the unknown.

> *The immediate population connection is this: a larger population generates a larger demand for potentially dangerous substances. It makes a difference whether (say) one billion or two billion people are releasing a dangerous compound into a finite biosphere.*

Freon (CFC or chlorofluorocarbon) came into common use in the 1930s and made possible the post-World War II growth of refrigeration and air conditioning; but it took forty years before two scientists discovered that it was destroying the stratospheric ozone that protects life from UV radiation. The ozone loss would not have been so great if there had been only half as many people using refrigerators and air conditioners.

Fortunately, there were workable substitutes for Freon (though they too may have unpleasant surprises in store for us. At least one of the substitutes is a more powerful greenhouse gas than Freon.) The shift to the substitutes was made with relatively little difficulty, but it can be much more difficult if we become dependent on new products such as commercial fertilizers and pesticides, because they can be justified as producing more food for growing populations. The argument is made that those substances must continue in use or people will suffer or starve.

> *If populations were not rising, we would not need to take a chance on unproven substances simply because they may help to provide for growing populations.*

If we are to get into synch with our environment, there must be a massive research effort to learn the potential consequences of releasing different compounds into the environment. The scale would dwarf the present scientific campaigns to conquer cancer and AIDS and to map the human genome. It would not be a short-term affair; more than one health specialist has warned us that it might be "several generations" before we become aware of the effects on human health of the chemicals we are releasing now. I think again of organochlorides and of Freon and that forty-year delay.

Such research may force us to abandon or redesign many of our industrial and agricultural practices. This could be an economic revolution far larger than the energy transition. And unlike energy we do not have any clear idea of the magnitude of the problem or the nature of the solutions. Those solutions, whatever they are, may turn out to involve major declines in productivity in some sectors.

> *We can accept a trade-off of reduced productivity for a safer environment if we do not need the productivity to support growing populations. The problems of commercial fertilizers and dangerous pesticides and toxic organochlorides may be just the prelude.*

> *There is a fundamental difference between two states of mind. If we are committed to growth, we ignore the dangers and precipitate the problems that science describes. If we conclude that growth itself is necessarily a temporary phenomenon on a finite Earth, we will be prepared to recognize its limits and inclined to resist pressures for uninformed growth.*

If population growth were reversed, humans and other creatures might be spared the unexpected consequences of our activity such as the horrors of future Minimata disease outbreaks, "mad cow disease" and its transfer to humans, learning disabilities, the unexplained proliferation of certain forms of cancer, and errors like the thalidomide fiasco.

X. BIODIVERSITY AND HUMAN SURVIVAL

The recent expansion and commercialization of agriculture, our alteration of forests and wetlands, our chemical assault on the biosphere, and our newfound capability for genetic manipulation will play out in complex ways.

Familiar Species. We worry about our destruction of species, but at a rather simplistic level. We don't want to lose the species we are familiar with, mostly mammals, birds, and fish. Under the Endangered Species Act, Americans go to great lengths to try to protect them. We seem incapable of understanding that we are losing their company primarily because we are usurping their environment. The solution lies in giving some of it back—much more than we have begun to contemplate in the creation of sanctuaries and biological reserves—and restoring their air and water. But we cannot do that while our own needs increase.

> *To belabor my refrain: the single best way to protect those species is to scale back our demands on the land and the economic activities that destroy them, and we are unlikely to get very far with such an idea unless we reduce our populations.*

The World of Microbes. By focusing on vanishing species, we are worrying about a secondary problem. The preservation of a healthy environment requires a much broader look at our companion species. Start, perhaps, with honeybees. Nobody has put them on an endangered species list, because they are not approaching extinction. But they are being harmed by insecticide sprays, to the degree that it has affected the pollination of plants in some agricultural areas. The question is, do our activities affect the ability of other species to play their role in the environment?

And that takes us to a much more important question. When do we begin to think about the microbes that maintain the environment in which we live? We are interdependent with the entire web of nature and (to our astonishment) particularly with the microorganisms we cannot see and that we did not even imagine existed until the invention of the microscope.

As Professor Lynn Margulis is fond of pointing out (to the intense annoyance of traditionalists), microbes are the most important part of the biosphere in maintaining the livability of Earth systems: "If you lost the animals and plants, you might lose the speed, but you would never qualitatively lose the cycle. If you lost the microorganisms, you'd lose everything; you'd unhinge the articulations of the biosphere."[44]

Humans vs. the Rest. The President's Acid Rain Review Committee raised the most frightening environmental issue of all in 1983. It pointed out that soil microorganisms are particularly susceptible to a change in acidity and warned that:

"It is just this bottom part of the biological cycle that is responsible for the recycling of nitrogen and carbon in the food chain. The proper functioning of the denitrifying microbes is a fundamental requirement upon which the entire biosphere depends. The evidence that increased acidity is perturbing populations of microorganisms is scanty, but the prospect of such an occurrence is grave."

That is a remarkably serious warning couched in the understatement of science. It is perhaps the nearest thing to a doomsday warning that has resulted from any environmental problem. Human activities could make the Earth uninhabitable by destroying the ability of earth microorganisms to stabilize the system. Unlikely—one may hope—but by no means impossible. Research has yet to dismiss that warning.

Any modern philosophy must take into account our dependence upon that unseen world.

We are all in this together. Including the microbes. I urge a widening circle of identification. Measure your belief and your actions against the question: How does this behavior affect the preservation of the Earth as a good place to live? Do my actions tend to help pass on an undiminished Earth?—Or better yet improve it for future generations? If the Earth is an interdependent system, does this not require solicitude for the variety of life, for the preservation of the complexity of Earth?

The Neutral Microbes. The microbes are pursuing their own interests and are not necessarily friend or foe. They stabilize the environment and the atmosphere, and they even protect us from our own excesses such as the headlong release of nitrogen. But other microbes like to feed on us, and they are doing very well. Our effort to defeat them simply encourages them to mutate, and they have a distinct advantage over us: they are prepared to accept heavy losses. "The microbes are challenging us in ways we wouldn't have imagined ten years ago and for which we're not prepared," said Dr. James Hughes, director of the National Center for Infectious Diseases at the Centers for Disease Control and Prevention.[45] We have not yet seriously begun to learn how to live with this cantankerous but essential invisible world.

> *Until we learn a lot more about our relationship with that microbial world, wisdom would suggest that we pursue the alteration of the environment with much more caution. Technology must not be under pressure to produce more food, or develop new toxins to deal with pests, or multiply the pharmacopoeia we already have, or tinker incessantly with the environment to keep up with rising human needs.*

> *A sane species, if it had the knowledge we have, would step back from this blind experimentation with our life-support systems. It would deliberately seek to move back to a level of economic activity that left much of the non-human world intact to buffer the changes that we inflict on it.*

Companions on a Small Planet. Of all the issues on Earth right now, perhaps the most fundamental is that we are in the midst of a colossal collision between biology and human growth. Growth had its place, but the Earth's living systems are being subjected to intense pressures because of the malignant growth of one part of it: the human species. Our success has become our failure. In the 20th Century, the world's population quadrupled from about 1.5 to six billion. Put it another way: we have added three times as many humans to the Earth's surface in the past century as we had in all previous time. And we seek a consumptive life based on new industrial and agricultural techniques (the Industrial Revolution) that multiply the damage done by sheer numbers. We are indeed a greedy tribe.

That growth has placed strains on the Earth's support systems unlike anything in previous human history. It has led to our usurpation of much of the biosphere that had been used by other creatures. And we are still growing.

XI. THE IGNORANT EXPERIMENT

More than one scientist has remarked that the human race is embarked on a vast, unplanned experiment to see what happens when we alter our environment. A refrain keeps beating incessantly in my head: we have changed the world more in the past two generations than in all previous human history and we don't know what we are doing.

The Danger of Linear Projections. All of us, including environmentalists, tend to predict in a straight line; twice as much of something has twice the consequences. Most things don't really move that way, because they generate synergies or feedback loops that accelerate the rate of change. Look again at the relationships I have been describing. There is a vast web of feedback loops, reinforcing each other to our disadvantage. LDC population growth requires more food and water. The effort to produce more food leads to forest destruction, which in turn affects the supply of water to grow food. The forest loss intensifies global warming, which in turn reduces food production and intensifies the need for more water. Fertilizers, pesticides, fossil fuels and chemicals all get us into comparable spirals.

> *We are almost certainly inducing changes at a pace faster than our linear thought processes can embrace.*

One potential non-linearity is particularly frightening. It was described by the IPCC: climate warming may induce fundamental changes in the pattern of ocean currents. The IPCC was thinking particularly of the Gulf Stream. By the standards of geologic time, the Gulf Stream is new. If it were to weaken or move, northern Europe might have a climate like Labrador. The circulation pattern of the Gulf Stream is presently under intense scientific scrutiny to gain some sense of its causes and what might change it.

Thresholds. We use the idea of thresholds as the basis for toxicity standards. How many parts per million or billion can people take without visible harm? I suggest that we apply the idea much more widely and ask ourselves: what do we know about the level at which the microbe, like the human, is measurably poisoned by the rising presence of different chemicals? What is the synergistic effect on beneficial microbes of the mighty cocktail of chemicals and minerals humans are injecting into the microbes' world? What level of soil acidity can the microbes tolerate?

This is a call for an intensification of scientific inquiry beyond anything presently contemplated, but the alternative is to gamble with our own future, without knowing the terms of the gamble.

Nations and industries are almost universally placing their trust in an endless series of best outcomes in the changes they set in motion. Nonlinearities and thresholds underline the opposite possibility: the danger of accelerated or abrupt environmental deterioration.

Delayed Consequences. Forest fires are ravaging the American West even as I write this book. At night, I have watched trees torching like matches on distant mountain slopes. The U.S. Forest Service estimates that five million acres have been destroyed in this, the worst American forest fire season.

I have mentioned scientists' warnings that we may not know the consequences of our actions for several generations. Perhaps we can learn something from this summer's holocaust.

Forest specialists are beginning to understand what has happened. In Ponderosa pinewoods, particularly, fire has always played a role, but that role has changed catastrophically since the European settlement. Traditional Ponderosa stands were open, the big trees scattered, the ground covered with grasses through which an occasional Ponderosa seedling managed to emerge. Grass fires swept through regularly, scarring the base of the pines but not seriously damaging them. Then, about 1880, in the Southwest, something changed. Sheepherders, cattlemen, and loggers moved into the stands. The fires suddenly stopped, judging from tree ring studies. The grass was eaten down, so the grass fires lacked fuel. With the grass denuded, Ponderosa and then fir seedlings began to grow, tightly packed. Eventually, they grew into dense, spindly forests "like a dog's hair". Then they began to burn.

There were no major fires in the Southwest until the 1950s. When they resumed, they were different and far more deadly, and progressively larger. "Ladder trees" carried the fire up to the crowns of the larger trees, and the fires became crown fires, so hot they are uncontrollable. Steadily, those fires have destroyed forests and the things in them, and that destruction may take one or two centuries to heal.[46] And, incidentally, they are contributing more particulates to air pollution and carbon to climate warming.

Would we have behaved differently if we had understood the consequences? I am not sure we would have, then; we have been rapacious about nature. Perhaps we would, now, as we slowly learn what we are doing to our own future. The experience underlines again the point: it may take generations before we understand the consequences of the things we do. The lesson, I think, is clear:

> *We must not push the system so hard, or rely on a best case scenario; we should reduce our environmental role sufficiently to forestall or accommodate the less favorable contingencies we may discover as non-linearities intensify the damage, thresholds are crossed, and we belatedly learn what we have done to the Earth.*

XII. THE END OF GROWTH

Charles Darwin and Family Planning. There is still a debate about regulating human fertility, because those who oppose it have not yet come to understand what the theory of evolution tells us about human behavior. Charles Darwin had a titanic role in the history of human thought. Out of his observations of finches in the Galapagos Islands came the theory of evolution, which explained things that had never been explainable before about population.

All successful species, he said, have the ability to bear more young than their environment can support. This enables species to recover from food-short periods and it enables the best adapted to expand and fill new environmental niches when the opportunity presents. It also leads to overpopulation and to the survival of the fittest.

That excess fecundity is central to the population dynamics of living creatures. It was true of human populations until we learned to practice fertility regulation by family planning. Like other animals, our population growth was limited by high mortality, particularly of the young. Medical and public health advances, sanitation and the growth of agricultural yields saved us for a time from that fate, but the process goes on. As human populations continue to grow, they will meet those limits. The Darwinian controls, imposed in part by our destruction of the ecosystem, will stop the growth.

Seen in that light, family planning is perhaps the most fundamental advance in the human condition. It permits the human species to control its growth by regulating fertility, rather than waiting for the control to come from misery and rising mortality.

Family planning is not just something that we are entitled to practice, independently. It is something that the Earth itself badly needs to escape the damage of continued

*human population growth. It is essential to the preserva-
tion of ecological balance in the face of a species grown
far too successful. Within our species, it is desperately
needed by the poor and fertile of the world so they can
escape the evolutionary curse of excess fecundity and so
their children will not be trapped in high mortality.*

We are threatening the very biological systems that support us. We can afford to do what a struggling endangered species cannot: accept our responsibility for helping to preserve the Earth's interdependent ecology.

The problem is that family planning is usually practiced for personal, not social reasons. Those who practice it are not asking, what is the optimum population? As I will describe later in the case of Europe, there is no assurance that the individual and the social interest will coincide and lead to a stable population at an ideal level. The very idea of family planning is not very old, and the idea of tying it to social ends is a new one in human experience. We are far from knowing how to do it. Defining an optimum population and learning how to reach it with family planning are central to any hope of an environmentally sustainable future.

Social Equity and Human Numbers. If we look forward to a world less divided between the very rich and the starving, we must expect a dramatic increase in GNP per capita, worldwide. If world population grows as expected, total economic growth must rise nearly tenfold to achieve such a goal, even on the best of assumptions (see my discussion of Economics above). That growth will be particularly malignant as the new industrializing countries put their heavy industry in place, probably without much regard to environmental concerns. But politicians call for faster growth, and their constituents applaud. In a linear projection, the stress would rise accordingly. But the impact may not be linear. It may accelerate as we continue to overwhelm our natural support systems.

I can visualize a society, even a planet, in which there is enough for all, and in which the poor can escape their poverty. I can see the possibility of a better life for smaller populations, but growing wealth for growing numbers is a certain prescription to worsen the environmental disasters that we are already generating. I will carry the point farther:

Put aside the endless speculation about how large populations will grow, and when. The nation and the world are already substantially overpopulated as we pursue the life style which the developed countries now enjoy and which developing countries would like to have.

Quantifying Reverse Growth. I have offered several indicators as to what population sizes might be sustainable. A satisfactory worldwide GNP per capita points toward a population of perhaps one billion. To get away from our risky gamble with fertilizer suggests a population of something like two billion. Avoiding man-made climate warming would become realistic with a population of about three billion. Any population reduction in arid zones would help to bring human needs into better balance with water supplies and would lessen the endemic overgrazing; populations one-third the present size would seem a wonderful relief, indeed. The uncertainties associated with climate change, and with chemicals and their impacts, suggest the need for a margin of safety beyond the calculations we can presently quantify.

Those are indeed very rough approximations, and they could be modified if humankind really embarked on benign solutions to its energy needs, but they converge on one conclusion: the need to move deliberately toward a much smaller population. That move would produce mutually reinforcing (synergistic) gains in all those areas. As with agriculture and forests, taking the pressure off one sector benefits the others.

We are already at war with the biosphere that supports us. More than any other proposed solution, a solution on the demand side—population—offers an effective way to end or ameliorate the problems I have described. It works across all those sectors, and, remarkably enough, it will save money rather than demanding more investments.

Europe's population growth is on the verge of turning around, and the almost universal reaction has been panic at the prospect—as if the population it so recently attained is essential to its survival. The reaction illuminates the general infatuation with growth. We heard few questions raised as population grew, but the end of growth is seen as a disaster. I think this topic needs more serious thought and a less visceral reaction.

The UN and "Replacement Migration." The popular press reflects the fear that there will not be enough labor to support aging populations in Europe and Japan. The UN Population Division has taken up the issue and has published projections showing how much "replacement migration" will be necessary to maintain (1) the present population, or (2) the numbers of working age people, or (3) the present ratio of working-age to retired-age populations, in several European countries, the European Union, Europe as a whole, Japan, Korea and the United States.[47]

The Population Division calculates that all the countries studied, except the United States, will need to raise immigration rates to avoid population decline. The most dramatic projections are those under projection (3) above: the immigration necessary to maintain a constant ratio of working age residents to those over 64. At the extreme, Korea would require more than 5 billion immigrants by 2050, raising its population to 6.2 billion, almost none of them of Korean ancestry. Europe would need 1.4 billion immigrants, for a population of 2.3 billion. For Japan, the numbers are 524 million and 818 million. And, although the point is not made explicit, the migration and populations would presumably continue to grow after 2050. The Population Division, by the very act of publishing such projections, evidently meant to suggest their absurdity and thereby make the point that immigration is not a solution to what is happening in those countries. The report points out that those are projections, not recommendations. By focusing on ways to maintain population and working age levels, however, the Population Division seems to have concurred in the general public malaise at a population turnaround.

This is a legitimate area for exploration by the Population Division, but I have three fundamental problems with the UN approach.

1. It implicitly treated maintenance of present populations as a desirable goal. (The subtitle itself suggests that declining populations require "solutions.") Projections (1) and (2) become largely academic if that is not the goal. The report would have been more balanced if it had acknowledged the gains to be realized from smaller populations.

2. The authors treat immigration as the only tool to address the aging of European populations, pointing out that "only international migration could be instrumental in addressing population decline and population aging in the short to medium term." In fact, as I shall describe later, the dependency ratios are favorable in the short term, population declines are a long term rather than a short-term phenomenon, and as the report itself makes clear, immigration is not a feasible long-term "solution." The report would have sounded considerably less apocalyptic if it had studied the demographic implications of a rise in fertility. (It touched only briefly on one consequence of a return to the fertility levels in the UN 1998 high projection.) That would have dramatized the importance of bringing fertility back toward replacement level, which ultimately is the only alternative to national submergence or disappearance.

3. The report would have been more useful and realistic if the authors had studied employment and its possible expansion, instead of falling into the "working age" trap. By looking at employment rather than "working age" populations, it would have focused attention on a vital question (which it touched upon only in one phrase): how do those societies get more of their members back to work?

The European Environment. Let me propose a very different view: a smaller European population will be good for Europe and for the world, and the transitional problems are manageable, if difficult. Recent world growth has put very heavy pressure on the environment. It has driven up the natural carbon, nitrogen and phosphate load in the biosphere, generating fundamental changes in the world ecology. It has led to water pollution and atmospheric acidification, and it drives the worldwide problem of atmospheric carbon loading and climate change. Europe and Japan are two of the most crowded regions on Earth. Western Europe has grown by 27 percent since 1950, Japan by 50 percent. With populations more like those of 1950, or even earlier, they could enjoy the benefits of prosperity without the environmental costs that have come to characterize it.

Europe is in a better position than most of us to plan for sustainability, because its population has stopped growing. However, it has some serious disadvantages resulting from past growth. Its environment is under intense pressure simply because it is so densely populated. For one typical example: sulfur oxide (SOx) emissions in the major European countries are much less than in the United States, judged by emissions per capita or emissions per dollar of GNP. But judged by the truly relevant measure of emissions per square kilometer, Germany, Italy, and Spain emit about twice as much sulphur oxides as does the United States.[48]

Comparable figures can be run on other pollutants. European forests are under more intense stress than ours are from acid precipitation and ozone, simply because the pollution is concentrated in such a small area. Pesticide use per hectare is triple ours. Fertilizer use per hectare in the European Union is twice that in the United States because they pursue maximum yields and pay inflated prices for food, which in turn leads farmers to use more fertilizer. Consequently, the rivers run full of the residues. The nitrogen load of the Thames is four times that in the Delaware River and 200 times that in the Nile. The Dutch and Danes must scale back a major industry, hog farming, because the pollution has proven intolerable. In Austria, 35 percent of mammal species are endangered, 37 percent of birds and 66 percent of the fish; for the United States, the figures are 10 percent, 7 percent and 2 percent.

A lower population will be a tremendous asset as Europe tries to come to terms with its environment. It will also be a major help in addressing the energy transition, because Europe is not well-endowed with fossil fuels or with wind-energy sites or sunlight for solar energy. Those who panic at Europe's population trends should consider those advantages.

Dependency Ratios. Those who are obsessed with the decline of the "working age population" compared to "dependents" forget that they are fuzzy constructs. The real question is how many of the people are employed? The proportion of the "working age" that is actually working varies wildly from society to society and over time. Many of the so-called "working age" people are highly expensive dependents, such as college students or policemen, firemen and retired military personnel retired at or near full pay. In Japan and to some degree in Europe, the standard public and private retirement age is 60, not 65.

Moreover, there is no very precise connection between dependency ratios and economic success. The present dependency ratios in Europe are supposedly highly "favorable", i.e. lots of working age people and relatively few children and older people—but unemployment is Europe's greatest economic problem. It drives the constant demand for more economic growth.

The Case of Italy. Let me use Italy as an example, because it supposedly faces a particularly dire future due to a declining population.

To keep the "working age/65+" ratio constant, says the UN report, Italy would need "a total of 120 million immigrants between 1995 and 2050 . . . an overall average of 2.2 million immigrants per year. The resultant population of Italy in 2050 under this scenario would be 194 million, more than three times the size of the 1995 Italian population. Of this population, 153 million, or 79 percent, would be post-1995 immigrants or their descendants."

Does anybody seriously think that Italy can grow to be almost as populous as the United States—that it would be environmentally bearable? Or, for that matter, that such migration levels would be tolerable? What those projections show most clearly is the limits of migration as a solution to an aging population.

Now let us take a more sober look at Italy's future. How desperate does it really look? Let me put it this way: only 52 percent of the "working age" population (15–64 years old) is presently employed, because of chronic unemployment coupled with liberal welfare and retirement benefits. By contrast, the ratio for the United States (adjusted to the same ages) is about 73 percent. If Italy by 2050 put the same proportion of its working age population to work as we now do in the United States, then 39 percent of the total population would be working—which is higher than the present 35 percent.[49] Those people, not the hypothetical "working age population", are the ones who support the rest. Some of the unemployed would be happy to have jobs; others presumably would grumble if they had to work, but the potential labor will be there.

Not a frightening prospect—if they can get those people to work.

There is a simple truism: an older population is an inescapable byproduct of the end of population growth, unless the growth is stopped by rising mortality. Unless they want to attempt the mathematical absurdity of perpetual growth, all nations will have to face that reality, and Europe is there now.

Europeans must decide to have more children again if their nations are not to disappear. Italy should be moving toward a smaller population but not so fast. A higher fertility rate would still lead to a smaller population, but it would slow down the aging process and ameliorate the problems. They need to ask themselves: what fertility level is desirable?

Let us examine three different population scenarios for Italy.

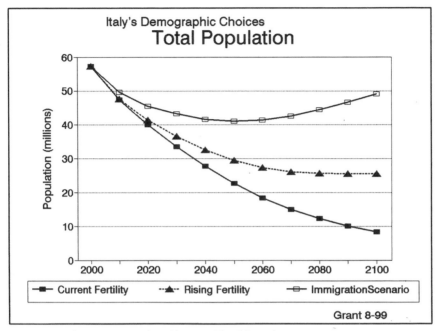

Fig. 13–1. *Italy's Demographic Choices, Total Population*

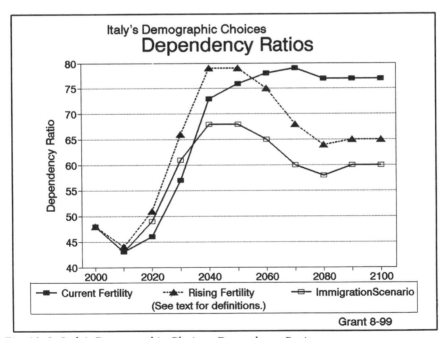

Fig. 13–2. *Italy's Demographic Choices, Dependency Ratios*

In the two graphs above, I plot Italy's population and dependency ratios through the coming century, using three different sets of assumptions:

1. *Current Fertility of 1.2 and zero net migration, with current mortality (on the assumption that decreased budgets for medical care—especially for the old—will counterbalance medical improvements leading to greater longevity).*

2. *Rising Fertility, to replacement level (total fertility rate or TFR of 2.05) in 2020, staying constant thereafter*

3. *The "Immigration Scenario", with annual net immigration of 200,000 men and women (in equal numbers), added to the preceding scenario.*

(Note that I am using the UN definition of "working age"—15 to 64 years. The UN study ignored the young dependents, on the grounds that on average they cost much less than old dependents. Following a more traditional approach, I have included them; they impose educational costs and hidden costs of job opportunities foregone.)

The Current Fertility scenario—or any scenario short of a fairly swift return to replacement level fertility—is indeed frightening once fertility has gone as low as 1.2 children. In Italy, current fertility would lead to a population descending past eight million in 2100—14 percent of the present population—unless immigration fills the decline. A rise to 1.6 children would lead to a population in 2100 of 15 million, and still declining. Given the intense migratory pressures generated by third world population growth and by the demands of employers in Italy for labor, extreme low-fertility scenarios would probably be overwhelmed by migration.

With zero net migration, the Rising Fertility scenario would lead eventually to a population stabilized at about 40 percent of the present level, which is not much different from the population at the beginning of the 20th Century. It results in a brief peak in the dependency ratio, but after 2050, the dependency ratio would begin to improve. That strikes me as a rather attractive scenario. The vital issues are, how do they achieve that higher fertility, and how much immigration will they accept if they do not? They may need to reconsider their traditional aversion to immigration—but at levels far more reasonable than the UN "replacement immigration" scenarios.

The Immigration Scenario holds the dependency ratio down. It preserves a larger population, if that is what they want, but it would transform Italy as post-2000 immigrants and their descendants become about half the total population. It is not unthinkable. Italy has gone through massive immigration before; Roman Emperor Trajan was of African descent. But that scenario would lead again to growth unless immigration or fertility declines.

Those are just three of an infinite number of possible scenarios.

Europe's Shared Issues. Italy and Europe will have real adjustment problems as the workers age. The problems will be more acute because of the speed with which fertility has fallen. But they are problems to be solved, not a fundamental threat. The medical care burden will increase, which may require that some benefits be capped. Early retirement and six weeks of annual vacation may disappear for a time. New arrangements may be needed, like matching older people with jobs suitable for them, or pairing up two semi-retirees to cover one job.

A world of free trade may become simply intolerable for Europe. It will be at an immense competitive disadvantage. Its workers will be in a position to command high salaries, but European products will be competing against developing countries with a labor surplus and consequently low wages. If Europe can manage that threat, European labor will be in an enviable position.

It will take a massive effort to bring fertility back to replacement level and to get more of their members back to work. It is by no means certain that demographic change can be engineered. Industrial nations have had notoriously little success in influencing personal decisions about childbearing, even where there is some consensus as to desirable family size. Moreover, under the Schengen agreement, Italy is part of a Europe with free movement of people, and the net flow of people within Europe is unpredictable. It has yet to be established whether the movement toward Europe can be controlled in the face of intense migratory pressures that are generated by the wage gap between industrial nations and most of the third world. In Japan, perhaps yes, in Europe, maybe not. Finally, there is no more evidence of a consensus about population policy in Europe than in the United States.

The present European experience shows the gains to be achieved by reducing population numbers, even as it illustrates the difficulties encountered when the shift is sudden. It is noteworthy that the problems of transition are much less severe in those European countries such as France and the United Kingdom that have come more gradually to population reduction. As a rule of thumb, a temporary decline to about 1.5 children achieves a population turnaround with minimal dislocation. Below that level, the problems increase.

We do not know what will happen to European fertility. Are the present extremely low fertility levels the product of women's sudden discovery of the freedom of "controlling their own bodies" (in the feminist phrase)? Will fertility rise as they get used to that freedom, and maternal instincts reassert themselves? Or are the current patterns more permanent? If so, how can women's choices be influenced?

> *But with all those uncertainties, Italy and the rest of Europe can celebrate the discovery that they are on the way to an environmentally sustainable future, unlike the rest of us. Europe is doing better than the rest of us in controlling its impact on global warming, to take one major current issue. A smaller Europe will be able to do even better.*

XIV. THE BLACK DEATH AND
THE RENAISSANCE

A changed point of view is slowly gaining adherents: growth is not benign; smaller can be better, not just from the environmental standpoint but in terms of wages, the standard of living, and indeed of civilization itself. Europe offers some historical lessons about the advantages of smaller populations and the transitional difficulties in getting there.

The Specter of the Black Death. For the Western world, the Black Death of the 14th Century is still remembered as the epitome of horrors. What we forget is that the Renaissance followed the Plague, and not by accident. The Plague fell upon a continent with a feudal system that had pretty much reached the end of its rope. The inefficiencies of the system and growing populations had combined to reduce much of the population to paupers. There was little dynamism and no incentive to improve. The Plague generated an extreme labor shortage, which rulers across Europe tried to deny by passing laws attaching laborers more tightly to serfdom. It didn't work. Surviving sons found themselves with doubled or trebled land and inheritances. The ratio of land to people suddenly improved, and farmers had spare money to spend and enough land to produce more and better food for the recovering cities, which were themselves stirred by the new opportunities as the guardians of the old system fell to the Plague. It was a time of immense dislocations, but a smaller and richer Europe produced the cultural flowering of the Renaissance. Though the Plague was a horrific way to do it, the reduction in pressure on the land opened the door to that awakening.[50]

The horror of the Black Plague lay in its method, not in its results. Population growth will stop. It will stop humanely through deliberate management of human fertility, or it will be stopped by malnutrition, rising mortality and surprises such as the AIDS plague in Africa. Better living standards may eventually result from either process, but the first process offers the hope of consciously opting for a better life, while the second depends upon the descent into misery to become effective.

Moreover, it is thoroughly uncertain whether the second scenario will lead to population collapse and then to a more favorable population ratio, as happened during the Plague and at other times in human history, or whether the outcome will simply be continued misery at the margin of survival.

> *The population policy advocate says, take your choice: is deliberate policy better than tragedy as the way to achieve a better life?*

The Irish Famine and its Lessons. Something of a repetition of the 14th Century experience happened to Ireland in the potato famine of 1848. Fed by that prolific new food from South America, the potato, the population had risen steadily until the crop failed. Then deaths and emigration suddenly halved the Irish population. But Ireland learned its lesson. The island's population was held down by late marriage and continuing emigration, and it is still only two-thirds what it was before 1848. Ireland has not had another famine, and today it is enjoying something of a boom. Migration is not a general solution in today's crowded world—populations must be regulated by managing fertility—but we can learn from the deliberate decision by the Irish to avoid returning to population growth.

Europe and the New World. 19th Century Europe provided a more benevolent example of population regulation in general. In that case the engine was emigration. The departure of perhaps 50 million workers for the New World raised the living standards for those left behind, but without the trauma of the Black Death. I have suggested that European labor in coming decades will have great bargaining power because of the present low fertility, if wages are not undercut by third world labor that has yet to enjoy the benefits of smallness.

Growth and Divergent Interests: Lessons for Moderns. The standard argument for economic growth is that it is necessary to create jobs. For whom? For an expanding population. It is a circular argument. Those proponents should consider the lessons above: the law of supply and demand works with labor, too. A shrinking population may reduce the demand for goods and services (and, incidentally, the attendant environmental problems), but it also increases the competition for the shrinking labor pool, and that translates into higher wages and improved per capita consumption.

Who benefits from population growth? Different groups within each society have divergent interests, and the self-interest of business and other groups is frequently antithetical. For business, growth is an opportunity for profit. The developer profits from growth, but a considerable body of literature is building up showing that the existing residents near the development bear much of its cost: roads, schools, hospitals, police, the whole infrastructure of growth.[51] Perhaps worse, they must live with the crowding that the development introduces.

Business seeks cheap labor, which is hardly to labor's benefit. Thomas Malthus two centuries ago warned the impoverished classes of England that "the withholding of the supplies of labour is the only way of really raising its price, and that they themselves, being the possessors of this commodity, alone have the power to do this." ("Essay on the Principle of Population") In other words, have fewer children. He was, however, deeply conflicted as to how they should go about it except by practicing sexual abstinence, which has not proven very useful advice.

Labor does not necessarily benefit when business is booming. Indeed, one study of English economic history over the past three centuries concludes that "there was an inverse relationship between social progress and growth... with ordinary people gaining most when growth was checked or slowed."[52] In the go-go United States economy since 1978, labor has been left behind, and the gains have gone to the rich. Real hourly earnings (the best measure of the earning power of the poor) actually declined from 1978 until 1995 and subsequently rebounded part way.[53] United States official income figures show the lowest 20 percent of households' real income substantially unchanged in that period, while income of the top 5 percent rose 60 percent—and that is without including capital gains, a mainstay in the earnings of the rich. The mean income of the rich thus rose to 24 times that of the poorest 20 percent, a ratio unparalleled in the industrial world.[54]

The growing disparity reflects something of a feeding frenzy among the rich. Massive immigration and the export of jobs have also driven it. With this combination, the largest businesses (the "multinational corporations" or MNCs) can go to where the labor is cheapest, or alternatively import cheap labor to displace expensive local labor and drive the price down, as businesses are presently doing in the United States, most dramatically with computer technicians and farm labor. In effect, the MNCs have been able to internationalize the labor market, to operate where it is cheapest, and thus to hold all wages down. Business and its followers herald the movement toward free trade embodied in NAFTA (the North American Free Trade Area) and WTO (the World Trade Organization). The purpose is to permit the free movement of capital, goods, technology and marketing techniques. Thus armed, the MNCs can produce in the cheapest labor market and sell anywhere. They can drive out local competition—businesses and farmers—by their combination of scale, operating efficiencies and deep pockets. They are not interested in population growth, one way or the other, but only in cheap and docile labor, but they profit from a world with too much labor because it keeps the labor cheap and docile. When local labor prices rise, or the docility erodes, they can move on. They leave a trail of wreckage as jobs blossom and then suddenly disappear in one country or another, but that is not their affair. They can evade environmental laws by lobbying against them or, when they lose, move on to more lenient countries. With the WTO, they have even established a judicial process to override national environmental laws that the WTO finds in conflict with international trade obligations.

This is a world in which all sense of moral obligation is overruled by greed and the pursuit of profit. Growth is immediately profitable, and ideas such as sustainability are simply beyond the time horizon of those with power. Our business and governmental leaders professed surprise when the popular opposition to their gigantic machine exploded at the WTO meeting in Seattle in December 1999. I will leave it to futurists to guess whether the opposition can crystallize sufficiently and for long enough to deflect the enormous political power provided by money and greed, abetted by the popular illusion that growth means prosperity. Business has plenty of followers. About half of American families are now invested in the stock market, and most of them presumably are eager to believe in the myth of perpetual growth—so long as the market keeps going up.

There should be a way for business and labor interests to be more harmonious—business does after all provide jobs, and business needs labor—but we have yet to find it. For the majority who do not profit but must live with the consequences of growth, perhaps the very inconvenience of growth will lead them eventually to recognize that smaller is indeed better.

Growth and the LDCs. The people of the LDCs would certainly benefit from a reversal of their population growth, and it is essential if we are to bring together the two worlds that are so rapidly moving apart. If somehow the LDCs could stop and reverse population growth, the misery in which so many of them live would be ameliorated—not just because they could stop destroying their habitat, as I described earlier—but because, like the survivors of the Black Death, each farmer would have more land and each worker more bargaining power.

That change would benefit, not just the LDCs, but the relationship shared with the industrial world. With the subsidence of the pressures to migrate, the rising tensions between migrant sending and recipient societies would lessen. If LDC wages could eventually rise to something like the average in the industrial world, multinational corporations would find it harder to play one against the other to drive wages down. Freer movement would be possible because it would not be a threat to workers in the industrial world, and the sense of a world in competition might subside.

But how do their wages rise? As Malthus pointed out so long ago, they have the power in their hands. We can now see more clearly than he did that it must be done through contraception.

If experience is any guide, family planning would reinforce itself, because it leads to prosperity, and the prosperous tend to have fewer children. The two worlds would not face each other in a zero-sum confrontation. Perhaps (to return to the case of Europe) both sides could welcome a moderate and managed migration to provide the bridge to Europe's future if European fertility does not rise.

> *The first and critical step in the process of untying this knot of problems is to jump-start the family planning that would bring the other consequences in train.*

XV. A NEW AMERICAN MIND-SET

How does the nation come to a new view of population and of its responsibilities to others?

The United States' Role in the World. The LDC leaders are much less wedded to growth than those in the industrial world, and much more aware of its dangers. They want to stop or reverse population growth. The question is why don't we do more to help them? In an interconnected world, it would be to our advantage almost as much as theirs. We cannot deal with the climate, or with global pollution, without all doing it together. And we cannot bring the Age of Migrations to a mutually profitable close.

The United States presently devotes less than 3 percent of its foreign aid budget to population assistance. That is 1/5000th of our national budget, or 1/25,000th of our GNP. Do we have our priorities straight? We have let our budget be dictated by a small group of congressional ideologues obsessed by the abortion issue and hostile even to family planning.

The Addiction to Growth. The leaders of the industrial world, including our own, need to learn that growth is no longer a solution to our economic and employment problems. The past thirty years have seen the beginning of widespread environmental awareness. Industrial nations have recognized some of the problems generated by the industrial revolution and mitigated them with technology and conservation. (Indeed, I would argue that the primary mission of technology today should be to undo the pollution and waste generated by earlier technologies.)

To believers in technology as a solution, however, I would say this: there are wonders yet to be revealed, and efficiencies yet undreamed of, but the pivotal question to ask of them all is, how will they affect the biosphere? Beware: one "solution" leads to another problem, as with fertilizer. And technical fixes become progressively more expensive and difficult as the easier ones are exhausted. Growth pollutes and distorts natural systems, and it must be met head-on.

I have argued for a vastly expanded and reordered commitment to studying the impacts of technology and human activity. I am convinced that such study would reinforce the recognition that the scale of that activity should be reduced, and its character changed. This is an area in which the industrial world and particularly the United States can lead. We should make what we learn available to others, and our own interests would be served by helping the others to develop their own capabilities. The science will be more persuasive to political leaders and the public if it is home grown.

The Cantankerous Americans. We are in a bind. Take a nation with a self-image of immense freedom; let it practice that freedom for two centuries; confront it with the dangers that our behavior poses to our own health and survival; and watch what happens. The hostility to "government meddling" grows precisely as the need for some sort of control increases. "I'll run my snowmobile where I choose." "My family has been grazing this National Forest for four generations; who are you to tell me I'm running it down?" "Don't tell me I can't use my backyard barbecue!" "This well is on my property; I can pump what I want." "I'll drive to work if I please. Alone"—even if it's 70 miles.

A nation of 75 million, in 1900, could tolerate a good deal of that sort of thinking. Our mega-nation of 275 million in 2000 cannot.

National Myopia. We don't see the forces that are driving us. I have collected literally hundreds of news stories from all over the country complaining about sprawl and the invasion of happy villages and rural areas by subdivisions and strip development and super-malls. Nobody sees that it is due to population growth, mostly from immigration, changing other people's way of life and driving them to invade your environment. The search for a better balance requires that Americans address the root of the imbalance—growth of human populations—rather than frantically addressing one or another of the symptoms.

Do we want crowding? Opinion surveys regularly come to the same thing: Americans like the sense of space we enjoyed for so long. By and large, we live in big cities only from necessity. You can't have it both ways: an open view of national population growth and the preservation of your own space. Or an immigration nonpolicy and a lower population. As cities grow, the effort to maintain a less crowded way of life leads to longer commutes on increasingly crowded highways, and to rising road rage. Sprawl is more than a linear function of population growth; it means increasing delays on the road, for you and the people that bring goods to the local supermarkets; and long commutes mean more hassle, more energy, more pollution, more climate warming. Fuel cells may help with the pollution and global warming, but they will be no help with the hassle. Or with the other consequences of growing national population density.

Remember where we were. Thirty years ago our political leadership warned of the dangers of population growth.[55] Perhaps we should listen, belatedly. I have described the shrinkage of arable land per capita in the United States. The same trend applies to our space, more generally. As we become more crowded, our environmental options—our hope of controlling our impacts and preserving the diversity of nature—are more and more circumscribed.

Fertility. How do we do something about it? It is conceptually easy if we recognize the problem and are willing to address it. Some years ago, I ran the numbers. If we were willing to embrace the two-child family and encourage mothers to "stop at two"—perhaps by adding inducements and disincentives to the moral argument—we could continue to have annual net immigration of 200,000. Yet still, within a half century the situation would have changed so we would face the beginnings of a gradual population decline rather than perpetual growth. Why? Because some women have no children and others have only one. If the rest stopped at two, the resultant average fertility would be about 1.5. In two generations we would have the luxury of asking: Okay, what size do we want to be?[56]

That projection would slip somewhat, in so far as women ignore the limit. In our rebellious society, to declare a limit is to invite a challenge to it, but it is really not such a wild idea. Already, about 70 percent of women have "stopped at two" or below.

> *I would argue that at the present stage of human growth the two-child family is a valid goal for people almost everywhere, though the Europeans could benefit from somewhat more.*

Migration. This essay began with the Age of Migrations, and I will return to that note. If we are to address population growth, we had better look at immigration from a longer perspective than is apparent in the current debate. Industrialists want more immigrant labor (meaning cheap labor); while more idealistic immigration protagonists say we owe others the chance our forebears had. Opponents point to the cost, the social strains, the threat to a sense of national identity and consensus, and the impact on wages, particularly of minorities and immigrants already here.

> *The debate usually bypasses the central point. The fundamental issue posed by mass immigration is demographic. It is the impact on our population growth. Two-thirds of this country's anticipated growth in this century will result from migration, and this will have profound effects on our environment and our dream of a sustainable society. Given the magnitudes involved, an effort to mitigate the population growth of the less developed world by absorbing it is to put us in their predicament, without making a significant contribution to alleviating their plight.*

We should indeed help others, but it is a questionable call for any American environmentalist to advocate unlimited immigration at the peril of continuing environmental damage in the one country for which we are directly responsible. We have an immense impact on the world environment. For the common good as well as our own, the United States needs to reverse its present inadvertent policy of promoting population growth. In our search for higher yields, higher productivity and higher incomes for more and more people, we are bending the environmental system progressively farther out of shape. We ignore the consequences of our policies, and then we apply Band-Aids and superhighways to try to compensate for the distortions we have created.

This has been a plea, not a model. Quite obviously, the demographic pressures vary from country to country, and each must tailor its solutions to fit its needs. I have not tried to propose how to divide a theoretical world population of one or three billion among different countries, since it would be a fruitless exercise. Each country, when it finally comes to a consensus that overpopulation is driving its troubles, will come to its own, perhaps unstated decision as to how much smaller its optimum population would be. A sense of respect for our shared planet would, however, suggest that those countries that hope to preserve high individual consumption levels should also remember that this should imply lower total numbers. What is good for the planet is good for the individual country.

I hope I have made the general case that, without a turnaround in population growth, we face some formidable problems. That does not mean that NPG is the solution, but it may be the condition precedent to finding solutions.

The Happiness Curve. I learned long ago about The Happiness Curve: the first investments yield the greatest rewards. They can yield great benefits in comfort and happiness, but eventually investment is simply an effort to catch up with a deteriorating life—like the constant turmoil of super-highway construction through and around our growing cities. In Hong Kong fifty years ago, I used to visit the New Territories, a lovely bit of rural China just across the mountains from the city. When I first got there, the Hong Kong Government was extending simple paved roads—two-lane blacktop—through those valleys. Bus services sprang up on the roads. The paths from the roads to the villages were paved. They were wide enough for a bicycle. I had to step aside as bicyclists came by, carrying big hogs on their backs, heading toward the market at

Taipo town. Those first investments were wonderful. They broke the isolation of the villages and made travel infinitely more pleasant than trying to negotiate the slippery paths through the rice paddies, particularly in the rainy season. And they made it much easier to get to school, to doctors and to markets.

Within two decades, that all changed. The pressure of population spilled over the mountain from Hong Kong. Big highways were built, and commuter towns. Weekend visitors poured into the lovely village "feng shui" groves, trampling them and killing the trees, bringing noise and loud music and leaving litter. The villagers hated it, but they were helpless. Within one generation, investment and growth brought first happiness and then urban sprawl and degradation.

Anybody who believes that growth is automatically good should have witnessed those changes. I could take my point farther with more desperate examples such as the intolerable conditions of the poor in growing third world cities. Bigger is not better. Ancient Athens, with perhaps 200,000 people, was at least as interesting and exciting a place to live as modern New York, with 20 million, and it was a lot less frustrating. They walked to the market, met friends there or in each other's houses, and climbed to the Acropolis for religious and political ceremonies. Amid what glorious surroundings! And it did not require that they tear up the Earth or displace other creatures (though in fact they did a bit of both).

With growth, we build more, but do we build better? A Gothic church and modern skyscraper use different techniques, but I don't think that the skyscraper is better. It is created, not by a vision, but simply by the need to build upward when overcrowding makes horizontal growth impractical. Is art better because there are more people making it? The Lascaux cave paintings of 15 millennia ago reflect draftsmanship and a compelling artistic drive that shames most modern art. I admire technology and use it, but the best technology is not caused by population growth, and much of technology simply serves to mitigate the evils that growth generates.

Why Not? Perhaps the strongest argument for NPG is "why not?" I have mentioned that limiting the demand side is often the cheapest and least painful solution. It is, in fact, positively beneficent. Very few people in crowded or arid areas would be likely to say there should be more people. By the nature of this exercise, I have emphasized dangers but, even if we discover that the microbes can handle a growing nitrogen load forever, or that there are wholly benign substitutes for organochlorides, a less crowded world offers spiritual rewards and a margin of safety for the unexpected.

It is not, after all, a terrible inconvenience to have two children rather than four, particularly since the low fertility countries have brought child mortality so low that there is little chance of losing them. Social insurance arrangements in the same countries have made children less important as individual "old age insurance"; and the Italian example above should reassure us that societies can handle the transition to smaller populations. I would not propose a fertility decline quite so drastic as Europe's, but I have pointed out that a tight labor market tends to drive wages up rather than down.

It might not be good for entrepreneurs or those who play on a rising stock market, but then I don't have to worry about them. They do very well without me.

1. See Negative Population Growth, Inc. (NPG), NPG FORUM "Climate, Population and UNCED+5," October 1997.

2. *The World Bank Atlas, 1996,* p.20.

3. UN Food & Agriculture Organization, Rome, FAOSTATS (computerized agricultural data base updated continuously.)

4. Pimentel '96. David & Marcia Pimentel, Eds., *Food, Energy and Society* (University Press of Colorado, 1996).

5. World Resources Institute (WRI), UN Environment Programme (UNEP), UN Development Programme (UNDP), *1998–1999 World Resources: A Guide to the Global Environment,* pp.42–46.

6. Copyright Environment News Service (ENS) 2000. All rights reserved. Republished with permission from ENS online at: http://ens-news.com. For full text and graphics please visit:

   http://ens.lycos.com/ens/aug2000/2000L-08-17-03.html.

7. FAOSTATS, see Note 2.

8. *World Resources 1998–99,* (see Note 4), p.186.

9. U.S. Department of Agriculture, *National Resource Inventory 1997.*

10. H.W. Kendall & D. Pimentel, "Constraints on the Expansion of the Global Food Supply", *Ambio* 23, 1994, pp. 198–205.

11. Reuters, Washington 10-9-1998, quoting the U.S. Geological Survey.

12. UN Economic & Social Council, Commission on Sustainable Development (UNCSD), *Comprehensive Assessment of the Freshwater Resources of the World,* E/CN.17/1997/9, March 1997.

13. Sandra L. Postel, Gretchen C. Daily & Paul R. Ehrlich, "Human Appropriation of Renewable Fresh Water", *Science,* February 9, 2000, pp. 785–787.

14. *Science,* March 24, 2000, pp. 2126, 2225–8.

15. Smithsonian Institution, "Ocean Planet" series, Judith Gradwol, Curator.

16. UN World Meteorological Organization (WMO) news release December 16, 1999.

17. U.S. Department of Commerce, National Oceans & Atmosphere Administration (NOAA) news release, quoted by CNN January 8, 1998.

18. ENS, Washington, DC, November 17, 1999 and *World Resources '98-99*, p.174.

19. *Science*, May 12, 2000, pp. 925, 1033–5.

20. ENS, New Orleans, April 19, 2000.

21. See L.Grant *Juggernaut: Growth on a Finite Planet* (Santa Ana: Seven Locks Press, 1996) pp. 61–76 for a detailed review of the IPCC study.

22. U.S. Department of Commerce, National Oceans and Atmospheric Administration (NOAA), National Climate Assessment, June, 2000.

23. U.S. Department of Energy, Energy Information Administration (EIA), *International Energy Outlook 2000* (IEO2000).

24. U.S. Geological Survey (USGS), *1995 National Assessment of U.S. Oil and Gas Resources: the Economic Component*, FS024–98. USGS, *USGS Assessment of Undiscovered Oil and Gas Resources of the World*, *2000*. Released March 22, 2000.

25 ENS, Brussels 4-21-2000.

26. ENS, Washington DC, June 9, 2000.

27. Personal communication with Dave Roberts, Assistant Vice President, SeaWest Windpower, Inc., San Diego CA, June 16, 2000.

28. U.S. Council on Environmental Quality (CEQ), *Environmental Quality 1997*.

29. U.S. Environmental Protection Agency (EPA), *National Air Pollution Emission Trend, 1990–1998*. Chapters 2 & 3. (Figures 6 & 7 are from the 1997 report.)

30. U.S. Environmental Protection Agency (EPA), "Light Duty Automotive Technology and Fuel Economy Trends Through 1999", October 4, 1999.

31. ENS, Washington DC, May 23, 2000.

32. ENS, Washington DC, 11-18-1999.

33. *World Resources '98–99*, p.181.

34. *World Resources '98–99*, p.183.

35. UNCSD '97, see Note 10, p.18.

36. *World Resources '98–99*, p.47.

37. UNCSD '97, p.21.

38. CEQ '97 (see Note 22), Fig.6-11.

39. New Mexico Environmental Department (NMED), Ground Water Quality Bureau, "Drug Residues in Ambient Water: Initial Surveillance", By Dennis McQuillan & James Mullany, 12-1999.

40. Copyright Environment News Service (ENS) 2000. All rights reserved. Republished with permission from ENS online at: http://ens-news.com. For full text and graphics please visit:

    http://ens.lycos.com/ens/may2000/2000L-05-08-09.html

41. W.T. Sturges et al, "A Potent Greenhouse Gas Identified in the Atmosphere: SF_5CDF_3", *Science*, 7-28-2000. pp. 611-613.

42. Copyright Environment News Service (ENS) 2000. All rights reserved. Republished with permission from ENS online at: http://ens-news.com. For full text and graphics please visit:

    http://ens.lycos.com/ens/jun2000/2000L-06-07-06.html

43. ENS New York 6-13-00.

44. Lynn Margulis, Professor of Biology at Boston University, "Gaia, A New Look at the Earth's System," in *Technology, Development and the Global Environment* (Mahwah, NJ: Ramapo College Institute for Environmental Studies, 1991), pp. 299-305.

45. Associated Press (AP), 4-27-2000.

46. *Science*, 1-28-2000, pp. 573-575; Thomas W. Swetnam, Director of Tree-Ring Research, University of Arizona, presentation to Santa Fe Forest Forum, 6-27-2000.)

47. Population Division, UN Department of Economic and Social Affairs, "Replacement Level Fertility: Is it A Solution to Declining and Ageing Populations?"; ESA/P/WP.160, 3-21-2000.

48. Organization for Economic Cooperation & Development (OECD), Paris, *Selected Environmental Data*, 1999.

    http//www.oecd.org/env/indicators/publications/htm.

49. U.S. Department of Commerce, Bureau of the Census, *Statistical Abstract of the United States, 1999*, Table 1374; UN 1998 middle projection.

50. David Herlihy, *The Black Death and the Transformation of the West* (Harvard University Press, 1997.)

51. Eben Fodor, *Better NOT Bigger* (Stony Creek, CT: New Society Publishers, 1999). See particularly Chapter 5.

52. Richard Douthwaite, *The Growth Illusion* (Tulsa OK: Council Oak Books, 1992), p.50.

53. *U.S. Statistical Abstract*, 1999 (See Note 42), Table 699.

54. U.S. Bureau of the Census, *Current Population Survey, March 1998*, Table H-3.

55. L. Grant, *Juggernaut: Growth on a Finite Planet* (Santa Ana: Seven Locks Press, 1996), Chapter 17).

56. L. Grant, NPG (see Note 1) FORUM "The Two Child Family", May 1994.)

WARLORD POLITICS AND AFRICAN STATES